THE BIG FIGHT

THE BIG FIGHT

(Gallipoli to the Somme)

BY

CAPT. DAVID FALLON, M.C.

CASSELL AND COMPANY, LTD
London, New York, Toronto and Melbourne
Printed and bound by Antony Rowe Ltd. Eastbourne

First Published *December*, 1918.

CONTENTS

THE BIG FIGHT

CHAPTER I

FROM AUSTRALIA TO THE FRAY

WHEN great historians with their learned pens shall come to set forth the complete story of the most sweeping and horrible war the world has ever known, I figure they may perhaps have need of such evidence, information and material as a man like myself can give. I mean a man who has been through the red hell of the vast conflict in places where it has flamed most fiercely, a soldier who has been eye-witness of its superb heroisms, its stupendous tragedies, scientific marvels, has undergone its tense emotional and psychological experiences, bears on his body its wounds, has seen at first hand, with the amazement all civilisation has felt, the cowardice, bestiality, utter moral abandonment to which a nation may fall in a mad dream of the conquest of the world.

THE BIG FIGHT

My name is David Fallon. I am of the County Mayo, Ireland. And I'd ask your pardon for a word or two by way of boasting in stating that my ancestors for a pretty long journey back into history have always figured in the man-sized battles of their generations. My father, a naturalist, rushed away from gentle scientific pursuits in 1870 to bear arms for France against the Prussians. And it isn't only because I'm Irish that I fought to get into this present big fight—and I did fight to get into it—but for the pertinent and additional reason that it was in France my father met Mdlle. Sarah Voltaire, who not very long thereafter became Mrs. Fallon.

And small wonder, with my boy's mind stirred so many an evening by the exciting stories of the Franco-Prussian battles my father and mother would tell us of in the glow of the old library fireplace, that I had no trouble electing the course of my life. I left the University of Dublin to enlist in the British Army. I joined a Northumberland regiment, Nov. 19, 1904, and the military examiners were not at first quite so enthusiastic about the performance as I was, for I offered them no Hercules. I was then only eighteen years old, a little under medium height and slim as a whalebone. A weighing machine as far as I was concerned escaped with the small effort of marking one hundred and ten pounds. But I was sound of eye, tooth, blood and heart, and so they cordially handed me my uniform—even if they did have to trim off the sleeves of the tunic a bit.

It is only fair I should say for myself that I was a rather good boy—that the temptations besetting youths in the army have never left their marks on me. Not, believe me, that I was a sanctimonious kid—a good many miles away from that. But I was lucky in having a keen love of athletics and a pride of achievement in many branches of sport. There's nothing like such a disposition to keep a boy clean and straight. Soccer, Rugby, swimming, wrestling, running—the opportunity for such games and contests was constant in the army and made me devoted to military life.

And boxing! Good heavens, the whalings I took! But by the same token, the whalings I handed out! There is no use my telling myself that just about here I should be content to hide my light under a bushel somewhat. I'll not do it. The fact is I rose to the dizzy splendour of champion feather-weight of the British Army in India.

Just a few words more in order to place myself at the time when the vast war began. I saw brief, uneventful service in China, then spent years in India, took part in many of the " hill scraps," sporadic uprisings of the mountain tribes, dangerous and exciting enough encounters we regarded them then, petty memories now; stood before Lord Minto, then Viceroy, in Calcutta, in 1908, and received from him the Indian Frontier medal, was promoted to sergeant-major, and with the rank of staff sergeant-major was detailed to the Royal Military Academy at Dunstroon, New South Wales, as instructor in athletics, general physical exercises, deport-ment and bayonet drill. This was my station when Germany began its brutal attack upon its neighbours.

And let me say right here that while in any event Australia would have made a sturdy response to Britain's call, what Germany can put into its long-stemmed, china-bowled pipe and " smoke it," is that were it not for the appalling, cowardly, barbarous crimes committed against the defenceless—the women and children of Belgium, there would never have been, as there has been, such tremendous outpouring of fighting men from splendid Australia; 400,000 of them out of a population of men, women and children numbering 5,000,000! All volunteers, you understand! It is the volunteer record of the war—not forgetting Canada's mighty showing of 550,000 out of a population of 7,000,000!

It was not until Germany gave atrocious evidences of her disregard of humanity, not until its army had stalked in its giant size, a red-stained, moral idiot, through little Belgium, crucifying old men and women and children to the doors of their homes, ravishing girls and women, murdering the parents who tried to protect them; not until this enormity of degeneracy had passed into the history of mankind, did Australia take fire.

I know, because at the very beginning of the war I was sent out to Sydney and Melbourne as a whip for enlistment—made scores of speeches daily in halls, parks, street corners and other public places. My hearers were many, and they were earnest and thoughtful but deliberate as well. Enlist-

THE BIG FIGHT

ments came and numerously, but not with anything approaching a rush. Your prospective soldier debated a good deal with his own personal interests before he signed up.

But after Belgium! The crowds I addressed took the arguments for enlistment away from me—made the talk themselves, swarmed to join. Social ranks broke completely and almost instantaneously. Everybody flocked to the army—artists, actors, lawyers, merchants, clerks, larrikins, miners and the men from the vast, open places of Australia.

Brothers are these last in every degree of character to the American and Canadian miners, ranchers, trappers, cowboys; they are big, lean, brave, boyishly chivalrous men, shy of women but adoring them, willing to play romping dog any old time to win the smile of a child or the pat of its little hand.

It must stand as one of the most picturesque features of the war—the great distances these men travelled to the centres of population to offer their services to avenge the slaughter of the helpless in Belgium and to fight for the honour, prestige and life of the Grey Mother of the Empire.

6

FROM AUSTRALIA TO THE FRAY

Take, for instance, John Wilson, gold prospector. He came out of the wilderness, fifteen hundred miles to Sydney, to join the colours; four hundred of it on horseback, one hundred of it literally hacking his way through a dense, trackless forest of giant gum and eucalyptus trees until he got to Bourke, whence, once a fortnight, a train leaves for Sydney. Thousands and thousands of John Wilsons made their way to the cities.

And from the distant islands of the Pacific archipelagos — Samoa, Fiji, Cocos — when the news of Germany's infamy seeped into the men far in the interiors—the traders and planters in oils and nuts, the hunters of birds of paradise—they came out through the swamps, paddled their way on jungle rivers laboriously but tirelessly, determinedly to the coast and put themselves aboard the first ships obtainable. There occurred at this time a great shortage in crews for these ships, so that some were threatened with being held up for days or weeks for lack of men. Many well-to-do patriots, amply supplied with funds to meet the expense of a trip in the first cabin, signed up as stokers, seamen or deck-hands in order to expedite the journeys from the islands to Brisbane, Sydney, Melbourne or other coast communities where they might join the army.

And the larrikins, the hooligans, "hard guys" of the cities, gangsters, youths and men of lives abandoned to drink, drugs and other vices—Germany's unspeakable cruelty in Belgium even stung such as these out of their indifference. In the early days of enlistment we had managed to win precious few of this class to the service. The majority of them had been sullen and derisive to our appeals to join the colours.

"Wot's all this flaming war about anywye? Blast the bloomin' war, I ain't got nothin' to fight about."

That had been the characteristic response.

But the piteous images of children with bleeding, severed throats, of tiny human bodies dismembered, of decent girls and women subject to the foulest acts of vicious cowardice, sent the larrikins to us seething with rage and resolved, as it was especially hard for men of this sort to resolve, to accept the strict discipline of army life for the chance to spill the blood of the horror-makers of Europe.

As to these same larrikins, if you please,

I would like to set down some more. Scrubby they came to us, most of them, pallid, under-sized, some of them wretchedly nervous from drinks, drugs, under-feeding, bad teeth, all manner of irregularities of life due to poverty, due to vice.

But, "by the living God that made" them, once you'd repaired them—fixed their teeth, fed them, exercised them, made bathing instead of a drunk a daily habit with them, once, in short, that you'd properly set them up, and—excuse the emphasis—but they made the damnedest best soldiers of the lot.

Not that the professional men, business men, open-air men who went into the ranks were not as heroic. A hundred incidents of the splendour of bravery that men of all classes displayed crowd my memory to take swift, sharp issue with the idea. But you see the larrikin—the designation used to be one of contempt with me but is something pretty close to affection now, and I should say with several other thousands of officers as well—comes to you with the devil's own experience of hard knocks. He knows hunger, thirst, the misery of cold, of pains and aches he has no doctor to allay. And I would point out that one of these boys who has survived such conditions with a physique left good enough to get him into the army, must have started life with the flesh and blood make-up akin to the steel armour-plates and entrails of a dreadnought. So when you take him and give him only half a brushing-up, the readiness of his response would (may I borrow the expression of an Ally?) certainly jar you. His face gets pink, his chest sticks out, the sneer he wore becomes a smile, the contemptible trickery he used to work turns to good-natured, practical jokes. He is childishly amazed to find that his comrades—the man who was a lawyer at home, or the other who was a tradesman or the very wonderful person who was a well-known feature in vaudeville and even—Gawd blime! his captain likes him. And once he believes that—knows it and feels it—then (another draft on an Ally) you've " got something! " The very gang training he has had when he banded with his pals to fight and cheat the law, that gang spirit with all its blind devotion is at the nod of his officer. He'll go to hell for you even when he knows there is not much or any chance of coming back; and if all of his kind, whether out of

FROM AUSTRALIA TO THE FRAY

Whitechapel, the purlieus of Canadian cities or the slums of Australia who have done that very thing of going into hell and not come back, might be called on parade it would be a big procession. Yet not of grief-stricken or agonised men, but they who walk with fine, clear, steady eyes, and countenances wonderfully cleansed.

To move a little ahead of that day in a then fast-approaching October when the first twenty thousand of us sailed away to get into the big muss, I'd like to tell a little story of the only larrikin I know of who fell flatly down on his job.

They had made him, to his fierce disgust, the Lord High Keeper of a carrier pigeon. He was a person who wanted to get into the fight—Anzac for Boche, yes, two Boches, or three. But here he had been made custodian of the carrier pigeon. He had never had a chance at a Boche. He must trail his officer, at the rear of charging men. He must have the pigeon in its little box ready, so that, should the officer command, the pigeon could have a neat little message as to reinforcements or success tied to his little leg, be released from the box, when he would shoot up straight as an arrow above the roar and smoke of battle and home his way to the rear, dropping into a box at the commandant's trench or dug-out station, and when he dropped into the box causing a very sharp-toned little bell to ring— a tone so sharp as to cut through the thunder of guns.

Well, one night on such a charge the officer missed his larrikin, and not long afterward the pigeon for whom the larrikin had so long been valet plopped into his little box at the commandant's dug-out, making the sharp gong clang incisively. The battle was roaring fearfully, but the commandant got the ring, retrieved the pigeon, slipped the little message roll off its slender leg, spread the message, swore first and then laughed.

" What is it? " his aide asked eagerly.

" I should," said the commandant, " have him arrested and shot, but I don't think I will."

" Who? "

" Capt. ————'s larrikin."

" Why? "

" Look at the message he's sent by the pigeon."

The aide read a message written in the heat

of the engagement, but with the stencil-neatness that larrikins acquire in the military schools :

"I am tired of carrying this dam bird and have gone into the fite."

[No signature.]

CHAPTER II

THAT carrier-pigeon soldier had my sympathy, for I had undergone his same sensation of exasperation at the very beginning of things. This was when I heard, back in August, 1914, that because of proficiency as physical instructor and drill master, it was the intention of my superiors to keep me at post at the Royal Military College at Dunstroon in New South Wales—keep me there to fit other men to go into the fight. I am no bloodthirsty demon and I am no brother to the Hun, but, having been a professional soldier all my life, what could you expect me to be but hopping mad when it would appear that I wasn't going to get in the greatest fight of history, when it looked as if all of the huge, smashing fight I would see would be from the side-lines? Surely that would be a great deal like asking a prize-fighter to accept a job as a dancing-master!

Well, I was Irish enough to battle for what I considered my rights. I kicked strenuously. These kicks got something of sympathy from my immediate superiors and so found their way higher, until finally I was in actual correspondence in the matter with Mr. Pierce, Australia's Minister of Defence. To him I set forth my case vigorously and often, and if he was, perhaps, somewhat amused at my insistence, he was just enough to take into consideration the good points I offered for myself, my long service, my Indian Frontier medal, and, in the end, to accept my own estimate, that I would be of greater value handling men on the actual front than being schoolmaster to the rookies at home. There were among the professional soldiers, I further pointed out to him, older men as able as I in training men and who had families dependent upon them, whereas I was not then thirty years old, and possessed no close family connections who would suffer materially if I should go the way that so many splendid, brave officers and men of my country and of France had already travelled—to the hospitals, the German prison camps or those rough-and-readily builded, nobly impressive, shell-swept graveyards which had come to existence in France.

THE BIG FIGHT

Now, perhaps had I been clairvoyant, had I been able to see ahead what was shortly to come—the savage, awful experience of Gallipoli, the murderous, weary days and nights in Flanders and on the Somme, the long suffering, the tremendous scientific ferocity of it all—well, perhaps I might not have tried so hard to bring the Minister of Defence to my way of thinking. And yet, while ducking the appellation of hero as I would duck a Boche bomb, after all, I think that with present knowledge of what comes to a man in this great war and what can come to him, I would still have tried for my chance to play my part in the great game. What soldier worth the name would not?

Well, soon enough there came a day that found us—the First Division of the Australian Expeditionary Force—on our way. We had no clear idea of whither we were bound. We thought for the most part that we were going straight to the fighting in France. There were thirty transports in all. My own crowd, about twelve hundred strong, were aboard the *Themistocles*, a converted White Star liner that formerly travelled between Australian ports and Aberdeen, Scotland, a goodly-sized ship she was of 13,000 tons. From every other port of size in Australia other troopships had come laden. At Sydney the entire thirty were mobilised, and with the Australian fleet, a complement of Japanese destroyers, and a French cruiser or two, we set forth on fairly smooth seas.

At all the ports where the populace got hints of the time of sailing of the ships there were great demonstrations, and likewise impromptu demonstrations of liveliest enthusiasm met us whenever we appeared parading on the streets, to say nothing of the crowd that came to cheer us at drill in our camps.

For, by October, Australia had come to know how tremendous and frightful a war Germany had planned, how viciously and hatefully Germany had resolved to strike at the very 'life of the British Empire, and Australia began to realise that if the British Empire went under, she herself would eventually have the Hun at her own throat.

It wasn't only the news of the mammoth operations which had started in Europe that brought this realisation. Things had happened " at home." The German propaganda, secretly, maliciously taking advantage of a democratic country's open hospitality, had effected bomb outrages, and worked insidiously to bring about strikes in the coal and iron mines, and strikes on the railroads, had worked the same despicable " below the belt" tactics in the Archipelago as she did in America. And the cables were constantly bringing news of fresh, cowardly outrages upon the old and the women and the children of Belgium!

The firmness of Australia's Premier, the effectiveness of Australia's police in its cities and of the Government's secret agents as well (once the German propagandists had revealed their hands) soon began securely to tie these same hands of the promoters of German frightfulness. But the people by this time had been worked to a towering rage, and as we started away in our troopships great crowds in the cities were riotously asserting their resentment. They wrecked scores of German shops, battered them into ruins, and put them to the torch.

With none of us knowing that Gallipoli was ahead we settled down to make our ocean voyage. Where, we didn't know at the time it was to take us, but we did make it as enjoyable as might be in crowded bunks and where we were for ever touching elbows on the jammed decks. Men never sailed on an expedition of war in better spirits and greater confidence. The regular soldiers and amateur soldiers were about evenly divided, but the amateurs were swiftly coming into line in physical fitness and expertness in drill. Still there were some funny incidents due to the novelty of the life that many of our men were leading. As, for instance, a little deck sentry, whom I approached one day and who looked at me and said : " Are you an officer? "

" Can't you tell that from my uniform? " I said, nodding toward the sergeant-major's insignia on my arm.

" Well, then," he said, suiting the action to the word, " I suppose I will have to chuck you a blooming salute."

We got together for all kinds of athletic fun—wrestling, potato and wheelbarrow races, running races, but principally the sport was boxing. Then there were serious-minded men who liked the sports all right, but organised a sort of debating society. There was no lack of interesting principals for this

THE BIG FIGHT

organisation. There were professors from
the Australian universities, Captain Knyvett
for example, who had been the professor of
psychology at the University of Brisbane, and
there were scores of his class. The debating
club discussed everything from Sanskrit to
how to fry an egg or bayonet a Boche.

One of two great excitements of our journey was furnished by "Bushy Bill," a reck-
less larrikin of Melbourne. Bushy declared
one evening a few minutes after dark that he
could do something that would stop the whole
fleet. We asked him what his little notion
might be, but he declined to tell. He said,
however, that he was willing to wager a pound
that he could succeed in his threat. Some-
body took him up, and the instant he did so
" Bushy Bill " put up his pound note and also
pressed into the hand of a friend all other
money and valuables that he had in his pockets
and without another word hopped over the
taffrail and into the sea. Naturally the cry
went up immediately of " Man overboard! "
Noisy signals were exchanged between ships
of the fleet, searchlights began to play widely
in all directions, and afterwards we learned
that in every other ship of the fleet, where,

like ourselves, everybody was on tenterhooks in expectancy of a raider's attack—the *Emden* possibly—orders were swiftly signalled for the ships to deploy. The *Themistocles* stopped and backed. Meanwhile two soldiers had gone over the side for the rescue of " Bill," believed to have been suddenly stricken with insanity. Following the two men who ploughed through the waves to his rescue, a boat was lowered.

Bill was all laughter and excitement when he was hauled aboard, enthusiastically claiming to have won the bet, which was promptly paid. But then Bill did some prompt paying. This was in the way of entering on a six months' sentence in the " brig," which held him for weeks also in the guard-house when our division got to Egypt.

Only the next day came a more thrilling event. This was when our wireless told us that the depredations of the vicious raider, the *Emden*, had been brought at Cocos Island to a swift end by the *Sydney*.

Of course, there was tremendous rejoicing. On all the boats, at all the " parades " (the assembling of the soldiers for afternoon drill), the news of the sinking of the *Emden* by the

THE BIG FIGHT

Sydney was "read out." Commanders made no effort to stifle the cheers that arose.

One of the boys composed a parody on "Tipperary" to celebrate the event, which we sang with greatest vim and vigour all the way to Gallipoli and afterward. It was worded this way:

It's a long, long way to Cocos Island,
    It's a long way to go,
It was there the *Sydney* met the *Emden*,
    And made old Kaiser Bill swear.
It's a long, long way to Cocos Island,
    But the *Sydney* boys got there!"

You can imagine that aboard this crowded ship, with men of all types and characters, and with all the rough play going on, it would not be just the sort of a place for a girl. Yet we had one aboard. We didn't know it for some time after we were out, because little Betty Grainger, in devotion to her sweetheart, had not only cut off her long, golden locks, but had deliberately roughened her hands with toil, the more to make good her disguise as a boy. Somewhere she had secured a uniform. In those days the uniforms were of all manner of irregularities; anything in a colour and shade of khaki would serve. The very style of military uniform belted with a skirt effect of the coat, and loose riding breeches, would enable a girl successfully to disguise herself. Betty did until one night when the men were playing a romping game of "tilt the cart," wherein your idea was principally to upset your neighbour by a quick grasp of the legs and a heave of him over your shoulder. When an unsuspecting rookie grabbed Betty and sought to "tilt the cart" she uttered a most unmanly scream. The men gathered around further to "rag" this effeminate boy, when Betty gave further evidence of her real sex by bursting into tears and scratching their faces. And then "Long Jack" Kennedy, of Melbourne, suddenly sailed into the men surrounding her, forgetting the camouflage that Betty sought to enact, picked her up in his arms, and faced the crowd with an outburst of oaths. That settled it—Betty, who had registered as George Grainger, was known for what she was. But even the authorities of the ship felt no bitterness toward Betty. She was given over to the care of a company of nurses aboard the *Themistocles*, and tried very hard to make herself useful, but because of the deception she had practised the commander ordered her to be put off at Perth.

We had a short stop and walk round Colombo and then at Suez. Four days later found us in an even stranger environment for Australians. We had arrived at Cairo—the first Australian Expeditionary Force, part of General Birdwood's army, which, besides our contingent, comprised the 29th English Division (regulars), the Zion Mule Corps, a detachment of French troops, four regiments of Gurkhas, several native Indian regiments, and the Indian Supply and Transport Corps. Although no efforts were made to put up barracks or permanent buildings, it was soon evident that we were to be kept in our Egyptian camp for some period of time. The magnitude of the commissary arrangements, the settlements of the regiments into a general plan of a large and permanent encampment, made this only too plain. We had all been hoping and cheering for our advent in France. At this time we were, as I believe, merely held by Lord Kitchener to further our training, for the conquest of Gallipoli—that red hell of disaster—was not in the books of our commanders.

24

FROM AUSTRALIA TO THE FRAY

German propaganda of the foulest and most awful sort swiftly made its appearance at Cairo. German agents had corrupted countless of the proprietors of the small resorts where liquor and gambling were to be found, had instilled all the inhabitants and keepers of bazaars in the native quarter of Cairo with ideas of secret assassination of our men for gain. Also, after the arrival of our soldiers, these insidious workers did all they could to promote an enmity between the natives and the Anzacs. The result of this campaign was sinister. Our men on leave were drugged and secretly murdered, their bodies made away with, with a skill that defeated all efforts at tracing the crimes. It is a fact that at least two hundred and fifty of the First Division of Anzacs encamped at Cairo never returned to their regiments, and no trace of what had befallen them, which doubtless was most sinister, has ever come to our exact knowledge to this very day. So thoroughly had the natives been instilled with an enmity toward us that the atmosphere and conditions between us became intolerable. The natives assumed a surly and insulting aspect toward us, and we in turn, I presume, swaggered and frowned and treated them with growing sharpness. With the full extent of the villainy that had been plotted and achieved against us, there came a night when resentment burst forth among a large company of the Anzacs and took the shape of a fierce, violent, and deadly reprisal.

The men secretly collected, armed themselves with revolvers, secured paraffin and oil torches, and some even took up bombs.

They rushed through the native section of the city, especially among its disreputable resorts, and did their utmost to destroy it utterly by the flames of their torches, and, where resistance was met, did not hesitate to use their firearms and bombs to kill. It was a night of horror in Cairo. But the crimes against us had been more terrible than the revenge. This summary and deadly action discredited the secret German agents and their influence and brought about from the natives a subserviency and desire to propitiate the Anzacs equal to their attitude of enmity before. It was a drastic measure that was taken, but under the circumstances it may be left to the judgment of the reader as to its justification.

FROM AUSTRALIA TO THE FRAY

There was intensive drilling in our cantonment, called Mena Camp, near the Pyramids of Gizeh, but just the same we found time for the indulgence in many sports, especially horse racing, camel and donkey riding, hunts for buried treasure among the sacred tombs of the ancients, and one party of the boys actually returned to camp with a genuine mummy for a prize.

But, nevertheless, life became monotonous, and we were all anxious and alert for an opportunity to show ourselves in the fighting. It was coming soon enough, though we didn't exactly know it then. But we realised that action was soon to begin for us when 10,000 men—500 of my own attachment aboard the *Euripides*—set sail under a convoy of twenty warships, including the great *Queen Elizabeth*—in the early part of April, for Lemnos Island in the Greek Archipelago. The physical aspects of this country were nearly identical with those we were to meet in the landing of Gallipoli. There was a vast promontory coming down to open water, always at a tempestuous degree, and there we went into a new form of intensive training. This consisted of lowering the boats in the choppy, stormy waters, landing the boats in the perilous surf, wading to our knees in water, swimming under the burden of our knapsacks, making numerous landings, digging ourselves in, and target practice at imaginary Turkish batteries, the real character of the batteries at Gallipoli having been discovered and reported by efficient British and French spies. When we were ready this was the order that came to us from our Commander, General W. R. Birdwood :

LANDING ORDERS

AUSTRALIAN AND NEW ZEALAND ARMY CORPS

April, 1915.

OFFICERS AND MEN :

In conjunction with the Navy, we are about to undertake one of the most difficult tasks any soldier can be called on to perform, and a problem which has puzzled many soldiers for years past. That we will succeed I have no doubt, simply because I know your full determination to do so. Lord Kitchener has told us that he lays special stress on the rôle the Army has to play in this particular operation, the success of which will be a very severe blow to the enemy—indeed, as severe as any he could receive in France. It will go down in history to the glory of the soldiers of Australia and New Zealand. Before we start, there are one or two points which I must impress

28

on all, and I most earnestly beg every single man to listen attentively and take them to heart.

We are going to have a real hard and rough time of it until, at all events, we have turned the enemy out of our first objective. Hard, rough times none of us mind, but to get through them successfully we must always keep before us the following facts : Every possible endeavour will be made to bring up transport as often as possible ; but the country whither we are bound is very difficult, and we may not be able to get our wagons anywhere near us for days, so men must not think their wants have been neglected if they do not get all they want. On landing it will be necessary for every individual to carry with him all his requirements in food and clothing for three days, as we may not see our transport again till then. Remember then that it is essential for everyone to take the very greatest care not only of his food, but of his ammunition, the replenishment of which will be very difficult. Men are liable to throw away their food the first day out and to finish their water-bottles as soon as they start marching. If you do this now we can hardly hope for success, as unfed men cannot fight, and you must make an effort to try and refrain from starting on your water-bottles until quite late in the day. Once you begin drinking you cannot stop, and a water-bottle is very soon emptied.

Also as regards ammunition—you must not waste it by firing away indiscriminately at no target. The time will come when we shall find

THE BIG FIGHT

the enemy in well-entrenched positions from which
we shall have to turn them out, when all our
ammunition will be required ; and remember,

> Concealment whenever possible,
> Covering fire always,
> Control of fire and control of your men,
> Communications never to be neglected.

(Signed) W. R. BIRDWOOD.

I am here reminded of an incident regarding this human, kindly commander that may
have a smile in it for the reader.

The Australians took pride in distinguish-
ing themselves by the wearing of an emu
feather (the feather of their native bird) in
their caps. No Anzac was happy without an
emu feather in his cap. I have already said
how willing and anxious the Australians were
to make good in their military duties, but how
hard it was for them to enter strictly into the
conduct demanded by militarism.

A certain sentry didn't salute General
Birdwood, who at that time wore no emu
feather in his hat, an omission the Australians
resented.

"What do you mean, sir," demanded
General Birdwood, "by not saluting me?
Do you know who I am?"

" No; who are you? "

" I am Birdwood."

" Then," said the sentry, without any loss of his own dignity, " why don't you wear a feather in your cap as a bird would? "

The general stared hard at the man for an instant, tried to frown, but laughed instead, and there was no court-martial.

CHAPTER III

GALLIPOLI

To-DAY all is quiet at Gallipoli Peninsula. The rows on rows of wooden crosses at Anzac and Helles, at Nibrunsei Point and Brighton Beach, look out over the Ægean Sea, doubtless blue as it ever was. The dead who lie beneath these little monuments of great deeds —the crosses amid the dwarf holly-bushes that clothe the western slopes—have reached their rest. In the scrub Lee-Enfields lie rusting alongside shattered Mausers. The pebbles on the long black beaches are mixed with shrapnel bullets, and in the sand and the dunes west of the Long Sap are buried bones and scraps of leather, clips of corroded cartridges, and shreds of khaki clothing.

We had no false idea when we left Mudros, eight transports carrying our particular 3,000 Australians, twelve more carrying the remainder of General Birdwood's division, as to the difficulty if not impossibility of the task ahead. Our training at Lemnos Island had shown some of the difficulties, especially the business of landing through choppy seas on narrow beaches under frowning cliffs and then scaling those cliffs. The Turks with their German officers had had their warning in the attempt to force the Dardanelles by the Allied forces in January. It was absurd to think that they would be surprised by any movement we could make only a few months after. We discussed the improbability of success quite openly. We went over the old defeats in the history of the Dardanelles, the defeats when Helen of Troy figured as the object of conquest, the defeats of the Crusaders and of Constantine. As I say, we didn't have much hope, but nevertheless, we were all glad that the time had come when the training was at an end and we were to go into the fight. Personally, I set about the same task as the others. On the eve of the battle I wrote to my solicitors, Garland, Seabourne & Abbott, as to the disposal of an insurance policy I had. I had no wife, sweetheart or parents, and decided to make an old and pretty crusty uncle of mine in England—he had given me a whaling or two when I was a boy—the beneficiary.

I had gathered before leaving Australia

ostrich and emu plumes and had made photographs of my companions, had purchased in Egypt the pretty little flower books made up in their pages of pressed flowers, had acquired sandal boxes, silk handkerchiefs and quite a quantity of " Turkish delight," as we always spoke of our tobacco. I made up many little packages as mementoes to girls I knew, to friends, and in common with the others gave them over to the postal clerk of the *Euripides*.

Of course, the world knows the fate of the *Euripides*, and so my will and all my packages of gifts and letters never reached their destination. But after the men had made these final dispensations of their little properties, had written their private secret hopes, fears, and expressions of affection to loved ones, the sadness of that period swiftly passed from us and we began to laugh and joke at the prospect of what was ahead. We even went so far as to make a sweepstake to be won by the first man to land on the Peninsula. We came to anchor at, I should say, about two o'clock in the morning off what we have since designated as X Y Z beach. This is at Kaba Tepe. The other detachments of General Birdwood's force were spread at anchorage up to and beyond Suvla Bay. The particular stretch of territory that we were called upon to capture was about five hundred yards long. It was a nearly straight line of coast. The beach was two hundred yards in width with a gradual rising of sand dunes tufted with dwarf holly-bushes and miniature tablelands, which finally resolved itself into sheer cliffs, some of them high and sharp like fangs, others rounded, in all giving the impression of the open, snarling jaw of some mammoth animal with scraggy teeth.

Our warships' pinnaces were launched and sent out to the different transports to take aboard the landing parties. Each man as we stood at parade on the decks before being ordered to the pinnaces had for his supplies as indicated in General Birdwood's orders, his rifle and bayonet, 150 rounds of ammunition and three days' rations, which consisted of his water-bottle holding a quart of water furnished by the clear springs of Lemnos Island, a tin of bully-beef to the weight of half a pound, as many biscuits as he could take on, while leaving room for his emergency tin which holds tablets of concentrated beef and cakes of chocolate. Besides, in his pocket he had his first-aid kit, a small roll of bandages and a phial of iodine.

Weirdly began our great and deadly adventure on this coveted stretch of the Ægean Sea, which if we could conquer made possible the breaking of the historic barrier of the Dardanelles. It was a stretch of coast we were soon to wash with our blood as literally as the Ægean's waves wash the self-same shore.

The long procession of transports and their grim battleship escorts had stolen up in the night, a widely spread yet organised, concrete group of slowly moving, black, gloomy monsters. Every light aboard each ship had been ordered out. Not even the pin-head glow of a cigarette might show on any deck.

The only light we had was the faint green gleam that filtered over the smooth waters from a moon that had begun to wane, and had indeed, at this hour of three in the morning, nearly fallen behind the ragged jaw of the black cliffs.

I can tell you that we most heartily wished this moon in—well, anywhere than shining just then upon this particular spot of the earth. We little cared for a moon to direct a spotlight on our surprise attack. It looked like an evil moon to us. Or, rather, it looked like the evil, watchful eye of our enemy. For all of us knew well enough what was behind those cliffs —about two miles or thereabouts behind. Oh, we knew well enough that there lay the Turks and their big, German-managed guns.

The Turks couldn't very well hear me talking at from four to five miles, yet such was the consciousness of the danger of our adventure and such the hypnotism of the scene that when I spoke to the comrade next to me it was in a whisper.

" I wonder," I said, " what that old green eye of a moon is looking at back of those dark old cliffs? I wonder if he sees the big guns drowsing and the garrisons asleep or——"

" What he's seeing," said the man at my side in a grumble, " is the heathen blighters getting ready to bang hell out of us ! "

" Cheerful beggar you are," I whispered back, the more gloomily because I was one of those who had argued and felt certain that we were not to take the Turks by surprise.

And now the men had assembled on the decks as soft-footedly as they might. They had gathered in the darkness into orderly rows like big companies of phantoms. The ships' crews worked as spectrally and nearly as silently as the lowering of ladders and the launching of the boats would permit. Even the groaning and wrenching of the chains and cables seemed subdued and ghostly. Small steamboats, each with a swerving tail made up of barges and small boats, panted alongside the transports and warships. With wonderful precision and swiftness the great ships spawned hundreds on hundreds of smaller craft, thousands on thousands of men, crowding the waters with them for as far as you could make out whichever way you looked in the faint moonlight.

"Fall in Number Nine platoon!" came the growled order.

That was my command.

I quickly had my men groping down the companion ladder. There were sixty in my special charge. By the time I had them all aboard and had stepped into the barge myself, where we huddled with fully two hundred more, the voice of our cocky little midshipman sounded. He sat most correctly erect in the stern, his cap at a jaunty angle, his slender neck in its broad white collar. He was so very young and boyish, but he had an alert and business-like eye.

"Full up, sir," he said smartly.

God bless and care for that gallant little chap! I can't help fervently wishing it as the memory of him comes to me now. He was only sixteen—the treble of childhood was still in his voice. But in it, as he gave his orders then and afterward as well when frightful peril came, were the steadiness and the coolness of a brave man—the sort of man he must have become if the dandy little youngster had not been destined for death with those many, many others on this April night.

The men in our barge, as it bobbed about, began to pass jests, in whispers of course. Not that they felt giddy—funny. Or, yes, in a way, a bit giddy—nervous tension, you know. Like a small boy whistling in the dark. And yet willing and eager to meet whatever dragon might be there. For now we felt and knew that all we had trained for, prepared for, thought about, imagined—the big time of actual warfare was at hand. That was what was most alive in every man's mind. But they joked.

"I've remembered you in my will,

Jimmy," said one to a pal two rows behind him. "You'll get nothing short of a million, my son."

"What—'cooties'?" demanded Jim. (I think I need not stop to describe "cooties," those "bosom friends" of the trenches.)

"Don't waste your millions on him, Bob," advised another. "Just leave'm a lock o' your 'air."

A small but very sharp voice cut in :

"Silence!"

It was the middy, but for all save the pitch of the voice it might have been a veteran commander.

"Cast off and drift astern," directed a basso from the transport's deck.

Our little man expeditiously carried out the order, and slowly we drifted astern until there came sudden twangs from the hawsers, startling because everything had been so quiet or muffled before. This was as the hawser coupling boats and barges went taut as each boat in succession, filling with men, drew suddenly to a halt its drifting predecessor.

Two of the men in our boat who were standing were caught by the jerk of the hawser and snapped overboard. They were fished out with boathooks under the rapid, cool direction of the indignant middy.

"Disgusting carelessness," he called the incident.

When all the boats of our string had been filled there came the order to the tugs : " Full steam ahead ! "

Our tug was quite ready for it. Our string straightened out in a jiffy, and we got off to a racing start—bounding, dipping and rolling. Sometimes we shot ahead in a straight line, sometimes in a half circle.

"God bless that damned old moon ! " said a man near me. His jumble of reverence and profanity came from the fact that the old green wicked eye of the moon had blinked out behind the cliffs. A moment before I had looked back and could see the cruiser coming on slowly in our rear with the obvious purpose of covering our attack.

Then I couldn't see a blessed thing. The green waters had turned to ink. You only knew your comrades were with you in the same boat by the press of their swaying bodies against your shoulders and your ribs.

About this time some of the gay Johnnies got another severe reprimand from our kiddie commander. They had undertaken to rise and were holding their bayonets out over the waters like fish poles, chaffing one another as to which of them would catch the first Turk. All said they wished it would be a particularly fat one—say, a three hundred pounder.

But the middy's eyes had got used to the inky darkness and he spotted the jokers.

"No skylarking, and silence all!" said the infant "vet." The men were pretty well on edge by this time. And, as the world generally knows, the Australian does not put much store in military discipline. But these men obeyed the little boy on the instant—all save one, who, though as quick as the others in resuming his proper place in the boat, disobeyed sufficiently to remark in a whisper, good-natured and admiring :

"Who'd 'a' thought we had admirals so blarsted young!"

And by this time we were within two hundred yards of the shore. A man near me voiced the impression we all were getting.

"Shouldn't wonder," he said, "if we're to surprise them after all."

Then suddenly out of that weird darkness, that curious silence that had been disturbed

only by the rapid, half-choking panting of the
steam tugs, the surge of the water against the
sides of the barges, the whispers, the occasional smothered laughs—all soft sounds—
there came hell—veritable hell if ever hell
comes to men on earth! And it came with a
tremendous roar!

CHAPTER IV

THE GHASTLY LANDING

THERE was a swift, sharp lightening of the
sky back of the gaunt, black cliffs, and our
boats seemed thrown out of the water, thrown
up into the air by the rocking thunder of the
heavy guns of the Turkish batteries behind
those cliffs. The water that had been so smooth
an instant before, that was, in fact, so
treacherously smooth, as had been the silence,
was stabbed and chopped and sent into wild
spume by a great rain of shells. Blinding
blasts flared as suddenly as here and there a
boat with its living load was struck and shattered. Screams and hoarse, impulsive cries
began to mingle with the explosions.

Then the cliffs and the sand dunes spat
deadly fire at us. In the darkness I could not,
of course, see it all. But it would seem from
what afterward I was able to learn that not
one of the pilots of the steam tugs thought of
turning back. I could not see it all, and had
no time to think of much other than myself

44

and my platoon a very few seconds after the bombardment from the big guns of the forts began dropping their shells and the hail of the machine-guns sang among us.

Surprise?

They had our range as surely as if we stood ten feet away from them. The water was cluttered with the accurate assemblage of their shots. Our ships had begun an angry, heavy retort, but whether their great guns were finding the marks, of course we couldn't know. It would have been a mighty comfort to us then to feel that these shots were smashing the Turks.

There was no indication of it. Their fire became more and more and more intense. Boat after boat was smashed. In not more than three minutes after the enemy began his bombardment against our landing, my own boat went to smash. A shell struck it at the bow. It shattered the boat and must have killed at least a dozen men. I, fortunately, was in the stern. With my comrades I was hurled into the air, and the next realisation was that I was far over my head in water and that the first thing I must do if I was not to drown was to get rid of my heavy knapsack.

THE BIG FIGHT

Thank the Lord, I had been a sturdy swimmer since childhood. I can't begin to picture to you how many scores of my comrades, unable to swim or weak swimmers, died then and there—how many of them with knapsacks on their backs and guns and bayonets in their hands yet remain at the bottom of the Ægean Sea, a curious spectacle for the fish.

I fought my way to the surface. And I clung to my gun and bayonet. I clung to them as frantically as any drowning man is supposed to clutch at a straw. For the only escape from drowning was to get ashore, and ashore I knew there would be small hope for me without my bayonet.

When I got to the surface other chaps were struggling all round me.

"Help each other get rid of these knapsacks," I yelled when I got my breath—"it's our only chance—or we'll drown like rats."

So we struggled about aiding one another free of these encumbrances. We had also to let our ammunition belts go and held on only to our guns. The shore was not far off now and we swam for it. But as we drew near—very near—within fifty feet or so, we encountered a devilishly ingenious snare.

The enemy had constructed on stakes in eight feet of water a barbed-wire entanglement along more than two miles of the beach. I was overhanding it for shore, supporting my rifle in the other, when I ran my face full tilt against the barbed wire's fangs. Others of my comrades did the same. They cursed and moaned. We hung on to the barbed wire, but ducking every instant, for a scream of bullets was all around us.

I can't tell you how many of the boats were smashed in the landing at Gallipoli. None, I believe, knows with accuracy. How many men were drowned outright none either can exactly tell. But there were hundreds. Nor how many men, exhausted, striving for the shore, were caught and held like netted fish in that barbed-wire entanglement will ever be known. That scores—yes, hundreds—were, I cannot doubt. Some of the men immediately around me I know were lost in the effort to get past it.

It was too closely netted to get through it. Some possibly floated or were lifted over it by the roll of the surf. I know only how I made my own way out of the trap. And that was by drawing myself down along the barbed strands until I found a space some two feet between the barbed-wire barrier and the sea-bottom. And I crawled through!

A few strokes after that and I was able to take to my feet and wade out. Well, hardly that. I plunged, stumbled, fell and finally crawled out on the bullet-spattered and shell-riven sands.

I wasn't paying the slightest attention to the bullets or the shells. Honestly, I was too exhausted. Had there been an enemy to meet me as I flopped on the sands the worst I could have done to him by way of resistance would have been to pat him on the cheek—if that much. I just flopped and panted and panted. And as my breath came slowly, very slowly, back to normal I was astonished to find that my rifle and bayonet were still clutched in my hand.

Fortunately, the enemy's own shells smashed their cunning, barbed-wire, undersea entanglement, and such sections of it as were not ripped in that fashion were made harmless by plucky bombing parties in man-o'-war launches.

THE GHASTLY LANDING

I didn't lay very long gasping on the beach, for the music of the bullets made me realise grimly enough that I wasn't out surfing. I staggered to my feet and began to take general notice. The boats that survived had spilled their men into the surf, and the men, huddling and scared, had nevertheless carried on. They were fast crowding the strip of beach. Officers were snapping out commands—heroically holding their presence of mind and organising their men. Organising, that is, what they could find of them, or any men, for that matter, that they could find around them.

All these things had now become visible in the dawn—the sudden dawn of the East. You must understand that the bombardment was ceaseless from the forts, the guns of all our ships roaring back at them the while. But it was the machine-gun fire and the rifle fire from the Turks concealed among the sand dunes and the clefts of the cliffs that were tearing our men down. Sometimes the big shells smashed holes in the beach and sent up great clouds of sand that settled blindingly down upon us.

Our landing party was grotesque and wavering under the frightful storm. Shouts, yells, screams of pain, cries of alarm merged into a great clamour. The most heartening thing, somehow, in the darkness had become the Australian cry of "Coo-ee!"—sharp and musical, in which men had called themselves together into groups. When the dawn came I was able to find twelve of the sixty men of my command.

There was no living on the beach. The only way out of that immediate hell was to charge across the sands and get into the shelter of the dunes, to fight our way to the base of the cliffs and get away from the shells of the cliffs, and to fight our way into enemy trenches in the table-lands and rout the snipers from their lairs.

Don't ask me how we did it. I am only prepared to describe how myself and my dozen men accomplished it. I wasn't, you see, exactly on a sight-seeing party.

In my little group of twelve who had been tossed into the ocean and made their way through the wave-submerged barbed wire we didn't have a thing to fight with but the cold steel of our bayonets. Our ammunition belts had perforce been abandoned with our knapsacks and were at the bottom of the Ægean.

THE GHASTLY LANDING

But His Majesty's warships were giving us a lot of aid. Their great guns were turned off the distant Turkish forts for a while, and their lighter armament was also brought into full play and together they swept the dunes and cliffs above us with a merciless fire. Actually we saw the bodies of our enemies, clusters of them, spouting from the places of their concealment, saw legs, arms and heads flying wildly in the air.

But back of me along the mile and more of beach there was a terrible litter of our own dead. And every minute somewhere near me a man was going down.

We got up those sand ridges any old way —by digging in our bayonets like Alpine staffs, clawing with our free hands, scrambling with toe-holds and fighting up on all fours.

We had just gained a knoll of sand and bush and taken protection behind it for a minute's breathing, when one of my men, one of those sturdy cattlemen who had made their way out of the wilderness to get into the war for civilisation, went down with a bullet in his leg.

" Nothing much," he said, as I bent over him to examine the wound, " and don't stop

for me. Go on and come back for me later,
or maybe the Red Cross lads will find me. A
little thing like this isn't going to——"

He was smiling as he talked, but suddenly
his head fell back, his smile widening into a
horrible grin. A bullet had taken him in the
neck. He was done for.

Of course, and luckily, there were only a
few of our thousands that had been blown out
of their boats, and most of the lusty fighters
of the landing force had their ammunition in
hand. They were going after the Turks with
rifle volleys of deadly accuracy.

Having come alive through the terrible
ordeal of that shell and bullet strand of open
beach, the Australians and New Zealanders
were fired to the highest fighting pitch. Companies of them sang as they climbed and
pushed and struggled along—sang or rather
yelled snatches of all manner of songs, though
they didn't sound much like songs. More
like strange, sustained savage war cries.

There was no staying the impetuosity of
some of them.

When we had gained the upper ridges
under the very face of the cliffs, and a furious
mêlée it was till we got there, orders flew from

the lips of the officers for the men to stop and
"dig in." The ragged sandstone cliffs were
pierced by hundreds of tortuous pathways, and
there was no telling what traps might lie in
these crevices and mazes. The enemy had
already given evidence that in tunnels in the
cliffs were located batteries from which had
come the most withering of fires until the warships' guns got after them. But beyond the
face of the cliffs it was foolhardy for any officer
to lead his men against an enemy save one in
full retreat. And although it was evident by
this time that we had the Turks on the run,
it was equally evident to our officers that their
commanders had been so confident in the
frightfulness of the fire upon the landing
parties and the impediments of barbed wire
they had planted in the ocean that they had
not massed a strong force in the sand dunes
on the face of the hills. The probability of a
much stronger force back of the cliffs practically amounted to a certainty.

And although we had the Turks on the
run, their forts two and three miles away were
still pouring their fire without an instant's let-
up on the beach and for half a mile or more
into the water.

But, in spite of orders, hundreds of our warriors refused to stop. They charged right on through the pathways and tunnels in the cliffs. We never saw them again. Those that were not killed were captured by the Turks. We used to say in speaking of them afterward that they had "gone on to Constantinople."

My little band, now numbering eleven, I brought together on a shelf near the face of the cliffs and we tried to dig in. But we had only our bayonets for implements, and the ground was a hard, brittle admixture of sand and stone. So, instead, I ordered them to gather a sufficient number of the chunks of rock that had been shattered from the face of the cliffs by the ships' big guns, and we constructed a horseshoe-shaped retreat—one that would protect us from the enfilade. In this we ensconced ourselves and looked from time to time on the bombardment, going as furiously as ever between the warships and the distant forts, with an occasional vicious spurting exchange between our light land batteries, which we had got ashore in the face of everything, and the hidden batteries that still held on among the cliffs. But mostly we snuggled with

54

heads well down below the walls of our little fort, for the bullets of snipers were pinging all around us. And you can imagine they had made things damned merry for us while we were doing our bit of architecture. The Turks at the time must have been pretty well demoralised, for let me tell you that, in ordinary circumstances, the Turk is altogether too accurate a shot. As it was, there was only one member of my little crowd who got hurt —a Melbourne boy, who had two fingers ripped off his left hand as he was shoving a big, ragged chunk of sandstone in place on the fortress wall.

Just as we had settled down to hold out until nightfall should take from us the uncomfortable job of being targets for snipers, I was startled by a big, horny-handed man in my company, a fellow with a cave-man's face and wicked eye. He had suddenly started blubbering. Before any of us could stop him, he jumped to his feet, showed himself head and shoulders above our baby fortress's walls, and shook his fist fiercely in the general direction of the Turks. Their snipers answered him with a furious spitfire of bullets. We dragged him down, and I demanded : .

THE BIG FIGHT

" What the devil's got into you, anyhow?
Want to get us all killed?"

" The little admiral!" he roared back at
me in fury. "I was thinking it was those
dogs and their guns killed that kid—I tried
to get to him when the barge blew up. Plucky
little devil! He was hanging on to the stern
and yelling orders to us to be ' Steady ' and
' Hold on.' And then another shell hit the
damn' thing, and he was gone." He tried to
get up again, but we held him down. " The
damn' kid-killing bunch of dogs!" he yelled.

But there were other hearts, yes, thousands
and thousands of hearts as staunch as the
" little admiral's " in that red day of horror.
There was the work done by the Australian
Army Service Corps—landing a steady procession of boats loaded with medical and food
supplies as well as ammunition, fleets on fleets
of these boats from the transports and warships moving to shore with the coolest regu-
larity, with the waters around every one of
them constantly thrashed by tons of falling
shells. Scores of the boats were blown up.
But the others never stopped, only where
there was a chance of rescue of the men flung
from the shattered boats.

THE GHASTLY LANDING

The stretcher-bearers and the doctors we could also see working calmly among the sand dunes, ignoring snipers' bullets as though they had been harmless flakes of snow. Slow and painful files of the wounded—those who could walk or stagger along were being guided to protected places until the coming of night might make possible their removal to the hospital ships.

As for the dead whose countless prone bodies strewn upon the beach with curious pitiful inertness so different from that of sleep, that you know instinctively means death— there was no use then risking live men to give the dead the attention, to award them such decencies of care and burial as were their due. This also would be the work of the night. Yes, and with many a man as he worked over the graves of his fallen comrades pitching into that grave, himself become a dead man—betrayed to a sniper by the moonlight's gleam.

Twilight veiled the sun, and then very suddenly black night came.

Well, we had done the thing, done what many men of authority had thought it would be impossible for us to do, what Lord Kitchener was afterward to describe as one of the most brilliant feats of bravery and soldiering of the war. We had effected a landing at Gallipoli. Perilously we were to hold our place on this narrow little peninsula, this back door of the Dardanelles, for months to come.

But at what a price! And through what suffering and horror!

Out of the 20,000 men who landed at Gallipoli by my own observation and all report, I do not think that 1,000 are alive to-day!

CHAPTER V

HOLDING ON

OUR little fortress or "sangar" could be likened to a cauldron, for it was constantly surrounded by fire—the bursting, flaming shells, and the pepper of snipers' bullets as the sharp bubbling of boiling water—to " carry on " the likeness to a cauldron. Down on the beach at the first ridge of rocky embankment the engineers had most bravely, under a frightful fire, blasted great dug-outs for the establishment of headquarters, a hospital, and the first station for the storing of supplies.

There never was an instant's cessation of the storm of Turkish shells from the batteries back of the cliffs, but other little companies like my own had gained a foothold on the first ridge and held on desperately.

Something like organisation was coming out of the chaos. My men were showing no signs of panic. I dispatched two messengers back to the beach to report my position, the number of men still with me, and to secure

E   59

food and ammunition. These men, in common with other messengers sent from similar small strongholds on the ridge, had a most dangerous duty to perform. They ran the gauntlet of intense fire. Many of them were killed. But my men successfully returned. They came laden with bully beef, biscuits and jam. Our emergency rations had disappeared hours before, and we were brisk enough in opening the boxes and tins and strengthening ourselves with their contents.

The organisation at headquarters went on with remarkable efficiency considering the stormy environment. I soon received a reinforcement which brought my reduced company of twelve men up to my original quota of sixty.

In the protection of night relays of messengers worked briskly in bringing to us rifles and ammunition to complete our supplies. Not that these messengers had any easy pathway. The storm of shrapnel was ceaseless and it was a bright night. We were as grateful for the ammunition as for the food, because, as I have already told, all the men of my detachment had been blown into the water, and in the saving of their own lives had necessarily abandoned their cartridge belts.

HOLDING ON

The Turks were still firmly holding a ridge some eighty feet above us from which throughout the night they kept up a playful attack of machine-guns, and their snipers were tireless. My men were so annoyed at these attentions that I had some difficulty in restraining them from making sorties. One of the men recklessly stuck his head above the rocky wall of the " sangar " and queried :

" Where are the Turks? "

" Over there," I said, with a nod toward the ridge.

" Don't they ever show themselves? " he demanded indignantly.

" Put your head down; get down, you chump, or you'll never live to see one of them," I told him.

Another time a sniper's bullet ricochetted around the rocky wall of the " sangar."

" What's that? " demanded one of my men.

" A ricochet," I replied.

" Don't we use them too? " asked that guileless rookie.

Fortunately for us the Turks on the ridge above were not possessed of bombs. They tried to make up for this deficiency by hurling at us huge chunks of rock that had been smashed by our naval attack from the face of their sandstone cliffs.

We made them a better retort. We took our bully beef tins and jam tins and tobacco tins laden with broken stones and cordite taken from our rifle cartridges, and messengers were dispatched to return with other forms of explosives and fuses to aid us in the completion of these amateur weapons of war. We lighted them from our cigarette ends and hurled them in whatever direction a Turk had betrayed his presence. Sometimes they would explode prematurely, and not a few of the bombers of that night had their faces blown away.

Dawn found us still in possession of the first ridge. While we remained there inactive, and before any order had been given to indicate that we were to assault the upper ridge, there came an order which aroused my wonder and opposition. It was to " Fix bayonets! "

Obedience to this order all along our position brought about a startling betrayal of the whereabouts of the entire force, for the sunshine glittered brilliantly on the steel blades and fairly telegraphed the location of all our quotas to the enemy above.

I knew there must be some mistake, and cried to my men : "Unfix bayonets! Who the hell gave that order? "

I never found out, but I have very definite suspicion. I am certain it was a false order circulated by spies, which we were frequently to discover were among us.

It is a fact that the German spy system even invaded the very personnel of the British Army. My platoon sergeant, Merrifield, summarily accounted for one of these spies. This was some weeks later, at the attack on Lone Pine. We had won the position and we were consolidating, improving upon the trenches and the strongholds which we had captured when the order came down from the left, " Retire to the first line ! "

I shouted : " Stick where you are ! Who gave that damned order? "

I sent up Merrifield to make inquiries, and as he was making his way along the line, asking the men where the order had come from, it was pointed out to him that a man on the left started the order. Merrifield went up to him and asked who gave that order to retire. This man replied : " Lieutenant Wilhelm." We had seen enough of spy work since we left

THE BIG FIGHT

Australia, and Merrifield, rushing up, faced Wilhelm. He did not stop to question him. He read in the man's countenance the appearance of a Teuton, the broad face, high cheekbones, and broad neck. And Merrifield took long chances, but was too enraged to consider that. " You damned square-head ! " he shouted, and with the utterance of the words killed the lieutenant with his bayonet. Wilhelm's attempted treachery not only cost him his life, but did not gain its end, for the order never got any farther. On examining his person we found letters, photographs and a signal code, all going to show that however recklessly he had acted, Merrifield had made no mistake.

The night of the second day found us in positions higher up among the sandy table-lands and ridges and dug into positions that we were to hold for a few weeks waiting for reinforcements which were coming up from Egypt.

The Turkish snipers occupied a great deal of our attention all this time, and they were a cunning lot. They were adepts in the art of camouflage—an art which was new to battle-fields at this time. Their favourite method of deception was to paint their bodies green, to shroud their heads with the natural foliage of the country, moss and holly-bush twigs. With this arrangement they could conceal themselves as neatly and completely as snakes in the grass. They not only hid in the shrubbery, but successfully concealed themselves in the stunted trees that grew among the rocky crevices. The cliffs themselves gave them a tremendous advantage. In this they had drilled shooting boxes—holes in all manner of secret recesses large enough to hold their bodies.

But we did not permit them to pot us wholly undisturbed. Many of our men made night expeditions that silenced for ever our hidden hunters. One of my bushmen came back from such an expedition with a startling souvenir. It was nothing less than the head of one of the Turkish snipers—the face of the ghastly object painted green, twigs enmeshed in the hair and sticking out of the ears.

But after a while we were to meet the Turk and find him not such a bad fellow. I asked the prisoners we captured why they were fighting. They said they didn't know what they were fighting for, but they just wanted

to have a fight. A rejoinder which an Irish-
man like myself could appreciate. In a conversation with an educated Turk I asked him
why they allowed the Germans to be their
master. He replied that the Germans had for
the last forty years overrun his country and
taken over the direction of the civil, the military, and the naval affairs of his nation, and
they were so strong, dealt with the Turks with
such an iron hand, that there was no commenc-
ing a mutiny. It had been tried and proved a
fiasco.

During the months of July and August
when the sun was very hot and the ground very
dry, and the flies and the mosquitoes were
everywhere, water became scarce, for it was
a waterless land we were on. The Turkish
prisoners, so friendly did they become with
us, went back to their own lines and brought
us water. We sent others back to try and
persuade their kind to come over and give
themselves up. We fed them well, gave them
the best that we had, and made jolly good fellows of them, as they were indeed. They had
given us a good fight, and we appreciate a good
fighter. Though they went back to their own
lines they would always return bringing with

them the gourds of fresh water. The water that we got ourselves was coming from Mudros and Lemnos. It was brackish, and it stank. We were only allowed one pint per man a day, a stingy ration under a tropic sun. The Turks said they brought us water because when wounded Turks lay gasping for water we had given them of our own.

Then the time came when we were getting an extra supply of jam, and there were only two kinds of jam issued—plum and an apple and apricot combination. Of course, that set us all grumbling, soldier-like, because we didn't get strawberry. One day one of the men hit upon the idea of exchanging this jam with wine with which the French soldiers were liberally supplied. This exchange went on for about a fortnight, and there were happy times in the trenches. Then the French got fed up with this sameness of jam and our stocks dropped below zero. So we had to look out for another customer. One of our boys hit upon the idea of exchanging the jam with the Turks. During the day we put up our articles of exchange—jam and bully beef—on bayonets, and held them up in prominent positions on the front-line trenches. And we waited anxiously as to what was going to happen, and lo! at night we heard and saw the Turks crawling through the brushwood and scrub, growling and muttering to themselves as their whiskers were caught on the twigs of the bushes. When they reached the front-line trenches they took off the articles of exchange and put in their place wines, cigarettes, and "Turkish delight," as we always called the tobacco. That showed us that they didn't want war, and we knew we didn't want war, but the Germans wanted it, and as long as they wanted it we had to keep going.

Likewise we had other experiences that were not all grim, but they were exciting. For instance, our bathing parties on the beach. We didn't have to bother with bathing suits or summer-resort regulations, but we had the novelty of bathing to the accompaniment of shell-fire. When we saw shells diving we dived to get out of the way.

Gallipoli at this period of the year was a frying-pan. Men found their uniforms intolerable. We cut our trousers into "knickers," abandoned our tunics, and did all our fighting in bare knees and shirt sleeves.

HOLDING ON

Our enemies got a wrong impression from this. Turkish prisoners told us that the report among them was we were falling so short of supplies that we were cutting our trousers in two to make double the number of pairs. The idea of our poverty of supplies was further strengthened by the fact that many of our men abandoned shirts entirely and moved about like savages, with bronzed bodies naked of all covering save the knickers and their socks and boots. Our aspect and the fact that our men went after them practically always with a bayonet, won for us from the Turk the respectful sobriquet of the "White Gurkhas," the Gurkhas being famous for their fondness and expertness in the use of the knife.

Not to give the reader too happy an impression of affairs as they stood with us in Gallipoli after the night of our desperate landing, it might be well to note here that of our original landing force of 20,000 there had been at least 5,000 casualties among us. The night of the landing in the storm from the Turkish forts, the cliff batteries, the machine-guns and the snipers, and also the drownings, fully 3,000 men had been killed or wounded.

THE BIG FIGHT

In the intermittent fighting of the following week's preceding the attacks on Lone Pine and Chocolate Hill, the work of the sharpshooters, added to that of many small engagements, had further depleted our numbers 2,000 more at least. We had held our own under these harrowing circumstances from the last of April until August, when the Second Division of new Anzacs came to join us.

In the fleet of transports that bore the fresh contingent of Australians and New Zealanders was the *Southland*, that was torpedoed in the Mediterranean. The men who arrived told us a most interesting story of the experience of the *Southland* and the 1,300 troops aboard her. It will be recalled that after being torpedoed the *Southland* had a remarkably long life. She was kept afloat for hours until beached on a rocky strand. The descriptions we got of the behaviour of the Anzacs and her crew were thrilling in the courage, cheerfulness and display of humour on the part of hundreds of Britishers, who had no way of knowing at what moment the wounded ship might plunge to the bottom of the sea.

HOLDING ON

One of the things they did was to hold an impromptu auction sale of the crippled *Southland*. Bids for the great boat, whose cost had been half a million, started at a shilling, and while she was being battered on the sand and rocks, rose to the majestic sum of one pound. She was knocked down at that price to an Anzac, who later, in all hopefulness, was to file his claim of ownership with the marine registry at London. He announced his intention after the war of taking the *Southland* back home with him to make of it an Australian bungalow.

The *Southland*, they told us, landed with her nose high in the air, and there was rivalry as to who should be the last to leave the ship. Men scrambled up the steeply slanting deck, clinging to rails, cabin doors, and any other object offering hand- or foot-hold. There were big bathing parties around the wreck before the men were picked up by the launches and barges from the other transports and warships. In the first of the shock from the torpedo, and when all were in expectancy of the *Southland's* going down, the men assembled on the decks and bravely set up the Australian song composed by a British naval officer, which had become dear to them :

Gather around the banners of your country,
    Join in the chorus or the foam,
On land or sea, wherever you be,
    Keep your eye on Germanee.
England's home of beauty has no cause to fear,
    Should old acquaintance be forgot ?
No ! No ! No ! No ! No !
    Australia will be there, Australia will be there !

CHAPTER VI

GIVING UP GALLIPOLI

IN looking over the notes and papers I have collected to aid me in the preparation of this book, memory is vigorously stirred by a clipping of an article from the Sydney *Mail* of October 31, 1917, written by a fellow-officer who prefers to remain anonymous. He wrote well of the familiar scenes of the famous battlefield as they would appear to-day. Following is an extract :

" The ' Vineyard ' has blossomed and the small green grapes cluster on the vine. The well by the fisherman's hut has run sweet once more. The cave-dwellers by Shrapnel Gully, Quinn's Post and Courtenay's are as quiet and still as tombs. Grass and weeds have grown over the winding paths that thread the valleys and scrape the hill-tops. The sandbags of the traverses have rotted and burst, spilling their earth on the litter of these battles of yesterday. And out through the chessboard field the grave-mounds of earth that we pattered down with spade and entrenching tool have blossomed with wild flowers and green grass. The warm, tideless Ægean washes these empty beaches where once thousands of men from the Empire's back-blocks made war as it had never been made before.

" Two years ago forty thousand men walked these paths. They slept in these dugouts, or in the trenches, and the detonation of the guns of the warships shook loose the earth and sand above them so that it rattled down in their faces, waking them from dreams of home to an uncomfortable reality. Think of those three days two years ago ! Think of the waterless fight for Chocolate Hill ; of the wounded lying in the brushwood and waiting for the sweeping grass fires to reach their resting-place. Men lay there unable to move ; some of them not able to pull their water-bottles from their web-slings ! Think of them and remember them, for in all wars there was never a more gallant forlorn hope than this one.

" Lone Pine, Chocolate Hill, Sari Bair and Biyuk Anafarta were goals set far ahead. Many reached them and never came back. Lone Pine was attacked on August 6, and of all the attacks at Gallipoli this was, perhaps, the most terrible. The Turkish trenches were supplied with head covers made of stout timber. Under these were loopholes from which the Turks fired with temporary immunity at the advanced Australian battalions. The enfilade fire was terrible, but the men bodily lifted the timber beams and dropped feet first into the dark trenches beneath. By 5.47 P.M., seventeen minutes after the first advance, we held the trenches. At 1.30 the same night there came a terrific counter-attack headed by scores of bombers. For seven hours the counter-attack pressed, wave on wave of Turks coming from the very parapet often to be shot and fall into the trench. One Australian brigade, only two thousand strong, carried this work in the face of an entire enemy division and held it during six days' counter-attacks. A thousand corpses were in the trench system after the occupation, and to make room for the fighting men these were stacked in piles at intervals between the traverses.

" There was one example there that will never die. The 7th Gloucesters lost all their officers and senior non-commissioned officers, but they fought on, mere isolated groups of men and the privates and lance-corporal, green troops of the New Army, from midday until sunset! The Lancashires, the Hampshires, Gloucesters, Australians, and New Zealanders—all did men's work in those days. None of their deeds will die, none of the names of men or regiments will ever be forgotten."

I was in the attack of Lone Pine which carried our armies nearest to the goal of capturing the coveted strip between the Ægean and the Dardanelles. I got my first wound of the war in the winning of these timber-roofed trenches, a bayonet thrust in the darkness ripping my right hand open, but doing my hand in the matter of its future usefulness no permanent injury.

Reinforcements had come to us till our numbers stood at forty thousand, but with the reinforcements also came aeroplanes, which later "spotted" for us the information that the Turks on the tops of the ridges outnumbered us by many thousands. They had also the support of the great guns of their forts, although our ships had made the contests in artillery fairly even duels.

GIVING UP GALLIPOLI

Lone Pine Hill was the most prominent ridge on our front. It was so named because the sweep of our fire had levelled a small forest so completely that only a single pine tree remained. Its foliage had been entirely blown away. There was left of it but its broken trunk and two gaunt limbs, blackened by explosions and upraised, curiously resembling the arms of a soldier in the act of surrender. We took this to be a good omen when on the afternoon of August 6 our orders came that on this night we were to mount these five hundred yards of rock, stubble and moss and possess ourselves of this highest point of the enemy positions.

We felt all confident. With reinforcements of our own Anzacs had come moreover big supplies of ammunition, machine-guns and additional artillery.

But also we knew the way ahead to be a hard one to travel, and our aeroplane observers in their reports and photographs had shown how deeply and firmly the Turks under their German officers had fixed themselves in the trenches on the summit of Lone Pine.

Nearly all the attacks up to this time had begun in the dawn. This time the attack was ordered immediately on the fall of darkness. The strategy succeeded. There is no doubt that a night advance was a big surprise, for we had made our way up along two hundred yards of ground before they suspected our coming. Then they flashed their star shells in the sky and swept us with a howling fire. It stopped us for a time, but we pulled ourselves together and held on until our commanders were certain that the Zion Mule Corps under Colonel Paterson, the famous Jewish contingent in this action at Gallipoli, were behind us with their sturdy animals heavily laden with the bombs that we already knew to be so vital a weapon in trench-storming. They used the mules as well to bring us additional machine-guns. But most of all we needed a chance to catch our breath. Our halt did not in the least mean our doubt of ability to get those trenches. It was part of good wisdom that our men should not attain the top of the ridge winded and exhausted from the climb.

We halted, crouching behind the rocks and knolls, gasping at first, for only about five minutes. Then we started to cover the rest of the climb and give the Turks and their German commanders " what for."

GIVING UP GALLIPOLI

The Turkish trenches, it must be understood, were built in the hillside, and their timber roofs slanted toward us. These roofs were honeycombed with loop-holes, from which their fire snarled at us as we came. Its first effect was deadly, but there was no wavering. Against the geysers of bullets these covered trenches were throwing up we simply went to work with our trench knives and bayonets, used them as crowbars and ripped the timbers loose. We blew the timbers into the air as well with bombs, although many of our men were disabled, being wounded by big flying splinters in the process. We dropped right in on top of the Turks and fought them hand to hand in their own dugouts. It was fast fighting, and we swiftly overwhelmed them. I recall to the reader as accurate the statement of the writer in the Sydney *Mail* that we captured Lone Pine Ridge in seventeen minutes of direct attack.

The Turks fell completely away from Lone Pine Ridge and retreated fully a mile across a shallow valley and on to another ridge, where we knew from our aeroplane scouts they had another strong position. In the judgment of our commanders we must be content to hold the elevation; the next advance, if it were to be undertaken, would have to be with the aid of tremendous artillery force in the taking of the great Dardanelles forts themselves.

From six o'clock in the evening of August 6 until half-past one the following morning you might have supposed that the Turkish soldier was a phantom for all we ever saw of him. But the batteries of the big forts never let up. For six weeks they were to hold us under a fire night and day. It wasn't exactly continuous, but you never could tell when it would open up, and never a day or night passed that did not find us under attack.

At half-past one o'clock in the morning of August 7 the Turks came back, seeking to regain the Lone Pine position. They fought us fiercely. They stormed their way against terrific machine-gun fire to the very brink of our trenches. Sometimes they actually got into the trenches themselves, and our men found them hard fighters in hand-to-hand struggles, and not like the Germans, as we were to discover later, cowards under the rip and stab of cold steel.

They were tireless in attack. We sent

back waves of them, but other waves came
on. They, too, had their battle songs, or I
should say song. It was always the same tune
they sang in swooping at us, a curious whining
refrain that would suddenly end in a high note
of ferocity or anticipated triumph.

There was a man at the end of the trench
that we had taken who did not belong to my
battalion, but who had jumped into the trench
suddenly with a whole box of bombs in his
arms and who before he got finished with that
night's work had won the Victoria Cross. I
saw him in the thick of a fight passing out
bombs with splendid strength and swiftness.
Besides, as I kept watching him he was tireless. He stopped rush after rush of battle-mad
Turks as they tried to force their way into
our dug-outs. Noting his effectiveness, I gave
orders to keep him well supplied with bombs.
I ordered two men behind him for relief, but
he kept constantly shouting back that he was
feeling fine and able to carry on. In the
morning that particular fight was over, and
around the section of the trench where this
man fought we counted forty-seven Turkish
dead. He wasn't scratched. My memory is
playing me badly at the moment and I can't

give his name. He was, however, sufficiently recognised in the official dispatches, which in naming him identified him as a famous cricket player of Australia. His bowling arm had certainly done noble work that night. Without the tireless stream of bombs he kept in the air at the enemy I am not sure that we could have held on to our particular section of the trench.

Official dispatches have told how we hung on to these advanced trenches from August until October, how the Turk was kept in subjection in so far as the territory we had so vigorously acquired. We settled down in the sandstone hills and grimly endured through these months an intolerably monotonous life.

We almost welcomed the blizzard that struck us in the latter part of October because of the change it gave us, that is to say, we welcomed it the first day when the snow covered the ridges and thousands of British soldiers turned into rollicking boys. We snowballed each other, we mixed our jam with the clean white snow, called it sherbet, and gobbled it, improvised skis out of the bottoms of barrels and shot over the ridges like human darts, built snow Germans and snow Turks and knocked them over, and one company created the greatest attraction by building a big snow Kaiser, which we bayoneted to pieces, with great shouts of laughter.

But we had to pay for this fun in the succeeding weeks in which the trenches remained frozen and the air bit into us cruelly. It was a big change from the blazing heat of the summer climate on the peninsula to the arctic weather that swept so suddenly down. And many new crosses were erected in the hillside cemeteries over the graves of men who died of pneumonia. Thousands were tortured by pneumonia and the minor infliction of frostbite.

Long ago water had become too precious a thing to be used for shaving, and our men had become as whiskery as the Turks. One fellow one morning, looking through his trench periscope, caught a reflection of himself in its mirror. He had grown a foot and a half of black whiskers, but hadn't realised the change it would make in his appearance. So he let a yell out of him to give us the alarm that the Turks were at our trench. But his own magnificent growth of black whiskers had deceived him.

THE BIG FIGHT

We lived so long in these trenches that were so much like rabbit warrens that we had got to calling ourselves rabbits, and one disconsolate man of mine that I found sitting in the trench one day and asked of him what might be the cause of his deep dejection answered :

" I am waiting for my ears to get longer and my tail to sprout."

I come now to a day in November, to be exact the 25th. This was to be an historic event for us Anzacs, and will doubtless rank as an historic event of the war. It was the visit of Lord Kitchener to Anzac, as we now call the two miles of Gallipoli strip we held. I am not in a position to make the statement authoritatively, but I think his coming was a complete surprise to the commandants. It certainly was to the rank and file. He arrived on a man-o'-war. Of course, great honours were paid him. The Turks were no longer active and the commanders had no hesitation in assembling fully 10,000 men on the beach to stand in review before the great leader. I was fortunately among them. I had, when in service in India (1906-1911), been a participant in the famous Kitchener manœuvres.

GIVING UP GALLIPOLI

I naturally looked at him searchingly to note what changes might have been wrought by the war and its responsibilities. He did look older as he stood before us—much older. He was a little stooped, but in the stride of his long lean figure he was as vigorous as I had ever seen him. And his eyes were keen and full of light and strength as he inspected us. It wasn't until days later that positive orders came when we learned officially that Gallipoli was to be evacuated. But he practically told us that fact that day. For a brief talk to the army followed his visit and inspection of three hours of the front trenches, his own observations with glasses from certain places of vantage, a submission to his consideration of all the aero-photographs that had been taken of the Turkish positions and strength, and a long conference with the supreme commandant of the period, Sir Charles Monro.

I will try to repeat Lord Kitchener's words to us as literally, as accurately as memory will serve. He said :

" The King and your country appreciate most deeply the great work you have done. To have effected a landing on this hostile shore and to have held it as splendidly as you have done is in itself a great triumph for British arms. I regret that the necessities of our armies, in conformation to other plans drawn, may not permit you to remain to complete this noble success."

And so Kitchener left us. His visit was not longer than twenty-four hours—in fact, the man-o'-war that brought him into Anzac Cove slipped away in the darkness some time before dawn.

But from that day we knew that all the perils and hardships we had endured in the fight for Gallipoli were to be crossed out in the record of results of the war. There began from November 26 a silent, secretive movement to effect our evacuation.

It must go down in history that this was most subtly done. If the Turks had ever suspected that we were thinking of withdrawing, they might have, in the last two weeks of the evacuation at least, swooped down and slaughtered the third of the force which was actually left on the Gallipoli strip. We used countless schemes of deception. To be specific, we would send away boatloads of a thousand men in the night, but in the daylight land boatloads of a hundred to fool the

Turkish observers into believing we were landing new forces. In the same way we would transport thousands of boxes of bombs and cartridges out of the trenches and the harbour in the night to the battleships, and in the daylight land from our barges, steamboats, pinnaces and launches, thousands and thousands of empty boxes that had contained the ammunition.

As we also withdrew our effects from the front-line trenches, our engineers displayed the greatest activity in making of all these trenches and barbed-wire entanglements the most ingenious of mechanical man-traps. Any force of Turks which attempted to swoop down the ridges against our slowly departing brigades would confront explosions of mines wonderfully camouflaged along the goat paths that were the only roads; to have passed through the barbed-wire barriers and in and over deserted trenches would have set ablaze other deadly outbursts of explosions. We also had set cunningly placed rifles on our outposts which would have been set off by any prowling Turkish scout, kill him in all probability, and at the same time give us an alarm.

We were not without our expressions of

sentiment in abandoning Gallipoli, for which we had fought so hard. We went among the rocks and heather and gathered wattle, otherwise known as mimosa, which is a sort of holly whose berries are yellow. It is the winter flower of the Gallipoli peninsula. We fashioned this into thousands of wreaths, and in the very last days of our departure placed them on the graves of our dead.

And, frankly, we had no great resentment against the Turk. He had been a hard fighter but always a fair one. He had always battled as man against man. Somehow his German officers had never been able to make him, if they tried, the barbarous, underhand, contemptible fighter into which I was soon to learn they could develop their own German soldier.

As a matter of fact, we left friendly signs behind. One placard read: " Au revoir— Brother Turk. Hope to see you again." Another placard read: "To Long Whiskers."

One dug-out showed a placard announcing: " Anzac Villa—To Let for the Season. Beautiful Sandy Beach all to Yourself. Splendid sea view. Home comforts. Lots of pleasure and excitement."

GIVING UP GALLIPOLI

Since Gallipoli German propagandists, with an idea of humiliating England in the world's opinion, have spread reports that if the British forces had held out a month longer we would have triumphed on the peninsula— that the Turks were on the verge of surrender.

Such reports are childish in their palpable falsity. As a matter of fact we were less than 40,000 men against 500,000. Against the great guns of the Turkish forts we had only in like artillery the great guns of the fleet. And the ships were being menaced by submarines. It is only for me to set down that the great Kitchener, going thoroughly over the situation, forced the evacuation that was so masterfully managed.

CHAPTER VII

COMPLIMENTS OF THE KING

" OFFICIAL documents "—the words convey the impression of dry reading—but I do not think those will be so found which have to do with the historic episodes of the landing at Gallipoli and its evacuation.

There is Lord Kitchener's message to the Anzacs, and in addition to its nobility and eloquence and the dignified State diction in which it was couched, there is the little addition of General Birdwood's, informal and affectionate, which touched us as deeply, made us feel as proud as did the message of His Majesty and Lord Kitchener.

This message, which came to us after Lord Kitchener had addressed us, and strongly conveyed without positively stating the Empire's decision of a withdrawal from Gallipoli, was as follows :

COMPLIMENTS OF THE KING

LORD KITCHENER'S MESSAGE

AUSTRALIAN AND NEW ZEALAND ARMY CORPS
Special Army Corps Orders.

November 25, 1915.

Lord Kitchener has desired me to convey to the Australian and New Zealand Army Corps a message with which he was specially entrusted by the King to bring to our Army Corps.

His Majesty commanded Lord Kitchener to express his high appreciation of the gallant and unflinching conduct of our men through fighting which has been as hard as any yet seen during the war, and His Majesty wishes to express his complete confidence in the determination and fighting qualities of our men to assist in carrying this war to an entirely successful termination.

Lord Kitchener has ordered me to express to all the very great pleasure it gave him to have the opportunity, which he considers a privilege, of visiting " Anzac " to see for himself some of the wonderfully good work which has been done by the officers and men of our Army Corps, as it was not until he had himself seen the positions we had captured and held, that he was able fully to realise the magnitude of the work which has been accomplished. Lord Kitchener much regretted that time did not permit of his seeing the whole Corps, but he was very pleased to see a considerable proportion of officers and men, and so confidently imbued with that grand spirit which has carried them through all their trials and many dangerous feats of arms, a spirit which he is quite confident they will maintain to the end, until they have taken their full share in completely overthrowing our enemies.

Boys! We may all well be proud to receive such messages, and it is up to all of us to live up to them and prove their truth.

W. R. BIRDWOOD.

Major-General A. Lynden Bell, Chief of the General Staff of the Mediterranean Expeditionary Force, issued the order for the evacuation of "Anzac." It was such as to take the sting out of it for us who had fought so hard, but must relinquish what we had won. I think it will be found as interesting a document as that which has gone before.

The Order of Evacuation read :

GENERAL HEADQUARTERS

December 21, 1915.

The Commander-in-Chief desires to express to all ranks in the Dardanelles Army his unreserved appreciation of the way in which the recent operations, ending in the evacuation of the " Anzac " and " Suvla " positions, have been carried to an issue successful beyond his hopes. The arrangements made for withdrawal, and for keeping the enemy in ignorance of the operation which was taking place, could not have been improved. The General Officer Commanding Dardanelles Army, and the General Officers Commanding the Australian and New Zealand and 9th Army Corps, may pride themselves on an achievement without parallel in the annals of war. The Army and Corps Staffs, Divisional and subordinate Commanders and their Staffs, and the Naval and Military Beach Staffs, proved themselves more than equal to the most difficult task that could have been thrown upon them. Regimental officers, non-commissioned officers and men carried out, without a hitch, the most trying operation which soldiers can be called upon to undertake—a withdrawal in the face of the enemy—in a manner reflecting the highest credit on the discipline and soldierly qualities of the troops.

It is no exaggeration to call this achievement one without parallel. To disengage and withdraw from a bold and active enemy is the most difficult of all military operations; and in this case the withdrawal was effected by surprise, with the opposing forces at close grips—in many cases within a few yards of each other. Such an operation, when succeeded by a re-embarkation from an open beach, is one for which military history contains no precedent.

During the past months the troops of Great Britain and Ireland, Australia and New Zealand, Newfoundland and India fighting side by side have invariably proved their superiority over the enemy, have contained the best fighting troops in the

THE BIG FIGHT

Ottoman Army in their front, and have prevented the Germans from employing their Turkish allies against us elsewhere.

No soldier relishes undertaking a withdrawal from before the enemy. It is hard to leave behind the graves of good comrades, and to relinquish positions so hardly won and so gallantly maintained as those we have left. But all ranks in the Dardanelles Army will realise that in this matter they were but carrying out the orders of His Majesty's Government, so that they might in due course be more usefully employed in fighting elsewhere for their King, their Country and the Empire.

There is one only consideration—what is best for the furtherance of the common cause. In that spirit the withdrawal was carried out, and in that spirit the Australian and New Zealand and the 9th Army Corps have proved, and will continue to prove, themselves second to none as soldiers of the Empire.

> A. Lynden Bell, *Major-General*,
> Chief of the General Staff,
> Mediterranean Expeditionary Force.

There was also posted for our information an exchange of telegrams between King George and Sir Charles Monro, Commander-in-Chief of the Mediterranean Expeditionary Force, which should also be given here.

COMPLIMENTS OF THE KING

From Buckingham Palace came the following to Sir Charles Monro:

December 20, 1915.

It gives me the greatest satisfaction to hear of the successful evacuation of " Suvla " and " Anzac " without loss of troops or guns. Please convey to General Birdwood and those under his command my congratulations upon the able manner in which they have carried out so difficult an operation.

GEORGE, R.I.

And the reply was:

December 21, 1915.

To His Majesty the King :

I have communicated your Majesty's gracious message to General Birdwood and the Dardanelles Army. In their behalf and my own I beg to give expression to the deep gratification felt by all ranks at your Majesty's encouraging words of congratulation. The troops are only inspired by a desire to be employed again as soon as possible wherever their services may be used to best advantage against your Majesty's enemies.

Charles Monro,
Commander-in-Chief,
Mediterranean Expeditionary Force.

And on the same date was received from the Secretary of State for War by Sir Charles Monro and duly posted :

THE BIG FIGHT

December 21, 1915.

His Majesty's Government received your news with the greatest pleasure and wish immediately to express to you and all under your command their high appreciation of the excellence of the arrangements for the withdrawal from " Anzac " and "Suvla," and their warm admiration for the conduct of the troops in carrying out the most difficult operation of war. They appreciate as fully the effective help which Admiral Wemyss and the Navy as well as General Birdwood and the Corps and other commanders afforded you. The thanks of the Government for this fine achievement are due to you and to all concerned, and I wish also to congratulate you personally.

CHAPTER VIII

AN INTERMISSION

In the evacuation of " Anzac " I had the honour, reserved for the men who had first landed, of being with those who left the tragic strip of territory the last. I was not a passenger on the very last barge, but, if I recall correctly, about the third from the last. We went aboard the transport *Andrines*.

I still had sixty men in my charge, but as I looked over them as they filed up the gang-plank into the *Andrines* the thought suddenly came to me—it really had not occurred to me before—that of all the men in my command there was not one of the original sixty who had left the *Euripides* with me for the landing at Gallipoli. Only twelve of the original sixty that I was ever again able to hear from had survived the blowing up of the barge and the barbed-wire obstacles. Of the twelve who had made my little company in the " sangar " we erected on the first ridge of X Y Z beach, there was not one left. Four had been killed, the others so badly injured that they had to be taken to "Restville," the hospital that had been organised in one of the dug-outs blasted in the stone ridges just above the sands.

It came to me that I also had not wholly escaped. My hand still showed the thread of the surgeon's stitches binding my wound received in the attack on Lone Pine. But, of course, this injury was trivial. It was, after all, for me a mild initiation to what was yet to come.

With a small convoy of torpedo destroyers, submarines, hydroplanes, our fleet of transports with about 30,000 tired Anzacs made Alexandria, where we were marched to "Rest Camp." It was just about what we needed after our strenuous months in Gallipoli. Some of our wounded were taken with us to Alexandria, others were sent to Malta, cases of shell-shock decided to be curable to the special hospitals in England, and cases that were despaired of were sent back to Australia, every effort being made in their transportation to get them home in time for farewell meetings with those dear to them.

As for myself, I was in the best of health.

AN INTERMISSION

And I was most eager to introduce a weapon of my invention—an armlet bayonet—to the army authorities. This effort, which took me from Alexandria to London, was not, however, to keep me more than six weeks from the big fight.

I had every reason by practical test to have faith in this armlet bayonet. It had a steel bracelet which fitted the forearm with an extension of two forks clasping the upper arm. On this brace was hinged a steel " T." The top of the " T " formed a bar to be gripped in the hand. The tail of the " T " was the blade of attack. This blade was seven and a half inches long.

My recommendation for it was that it was an ideal weapon for the hand-to-hand fighting which trench warfare and patrol encounters were constantly demanding. It had its special adaptation for English and Anzacs, all of whom have some knowledge of boxing, just as it would also be admirable for American fighters, with whom boxing is familiar from boyhood.

I knew that the Gurkhas, when they got at the Germans in the first part of the war, using their short knives, demoralised them.

THE BIG FIGHT

The German is not a natural boxer, and his gymnasiums give him no training in this art of self-defence. He is too much of an automaton ever to make a boxer. Thus, I figured my armlet bayonet would be a weapon invaluable in engagements where men came hand to hand, especially the surprise engagements of night raids in No Man's Land. This I had myself shown to my own satisfaction by actual experience. And the use of this new and, as it were, " surprise " weapon met its due appreciation in mention in Government dispatches.

But when it came to securing its formal adoption by the Government, I had a disappointment. I received permission from General Birdwood to present the matter to the Australian Minister of Defence, and was given the necessary authority to proceed to England and put my weapon before the Imperial authorities in London.

There I saw Colonel Buckley, Australian military adviser, who was keenly interested, and brought it to the notice of the chiefs of the Bureau of Trench Inventions. Colonel Burns of this bureau gave the weapon his hearty endorsement, but said the Government had no facilities, so entirely was every means already commandeered, to produce these special weapons in any great number. He advised me, if my means availed, to have some privately manufactured for use in future training of trench fighters, and said that the Government would gladly purchase them.

This I did within two weeks, having meanwhile had the honour of receiving a commission as lieutenant in the army, and, with this promotion from the ranks, being assigned to the historic Oxford and Bucks Light Infantry. The regular battalions of this old regiment were already in France, but my assignment was to assist in the training of the reserve battalions.

My special duty was the training of two hundred and fifty young Jews, mostly from London, who had been brought into service through the patriotic endeavours of Major Lionel Rothschild. They were boys from all walks of life, rich lads and poor lads, and their race can be most justly proud of their subsequent performances.

They were as keenly patriotic as any Englishmen could be, and although with few exceptions war was not an occupation of which they would have made a choice, they were convinced of their duty to defend the country, of the gravity of the situation, and were therefore very eager and wonderfully quick to learn. I had the armlet bayonet of my invention made in sufficient quantities to supply them all and gave them special instruction in its use, and they were afterwards to make frequent demonstrations of its effectiveness.

When these Jewish boys went into action their courage was splendid. I could write sufficient to make another book if I were to set down the individual stories of their bravery and devotion. Perhaps I can do them ample justice, however, with the simple statement that of the two hundred and fifty who flung themselves into the trench fighting in France, there were, when I was sent home crippled in the winter of 1916, but thirty survivors.

Their training with the other battalions of the Oxford and Bucks was conducted at Windmill Hill, Salisbury Plain. The Government always respects the religious faith of its soldiers. It is particular that military life shall not prevent proper observance of creed. The Jewish boys had their rabbi, had their opportunities to observe their fasts and feast days, and were fed in a manner ordered by the orthodox regulations of their faith.

I had had them under my instruction only four weeks when orders came for sailing to Europe, and I soon, therefore, found myself back on the battlefield—this time of Flanders.

CHAPTER IX

HUN BEASTLINESS

I WAS soon to find out the difference between fighting Turks and fighting Germans. The Turk will fight you like the devil, but he is a sportsman. He is incapable of the treacheries and ghoulish tricks of the German. He abhors attacking the helpless. I say this with full knowledge of the Armenian cruelties and outrages. I can only speak of my own observation. I am writing of how the Turks behaved in Gallipoli. One of my best men was murdered because I had been deceived into showing mercy to a group of Germans in a dug-out. Germans falsely surrendering, with hands upraised and whining cries of "Kamerad," had formed behind a small company of mine and sought to stab us in the back. In these next two months I was to be an eyewitness to the truth of the many accusations that the Germans were guilty of atrocities fit to burn horror into human minds for ever.

The reserve battalion of the Oxford and

HUN BEASTLINESS

Bucks with other battalions left Southampton on the troopship *Alexandria*, our military destination being Rouen. There were several other troopships in our company, a brisk convoy of cruisers and destroyers, and over-head a humming fleet of seaplanes. But the only thing that attacked us on the way over was sea-sickness. It is a marvel of the British Navy that no disaster has ever come upon these movements of her fighting men across the Channel.

One of the boys of my Jewish company was especially a victim of *mal de mer*. He had been a professional legerdemain artist in the London music halls. He said ruefully that he had never in his life brought so many things out of a hat as he had out of himself on the journey over. He said mournfully that he was anxious to fight Germans, but would have much preferred that they had come to England to get into the ring.

We landed at Havre, to an enthusiastic welcome from old men, women and children. The old men cheered us, the women wept, and the children scampered about our legs, throwing kisses, and with irresistible smiles, shouted :

THE BIG FIGHT

" Bon jour! Bon jour! Oh, bully beef! Oh, biscuits! "

If there is one thing that has rung the gong of popularity in France it is our English bully beef. And next to that our biscuits. And what could we do but share our beef and biscuits with those kids with the wonderful smiles!

Old men, women and children had all apparently learned the English slogan, " Are we down-hearted? No! " They yelled it at us both joyfully and tearfully, and we yelled back at them with vigour, " *NO! NO! NO!* "

Military transportation was working as smoothly as oil, and without delay my own contingent and some 3,000 others were rolled along to Rouen. We were sent to camp No. 55, Infantry Base Depot, a part of the 48th Division Territorials, Sixth Army Corps, Major-General Fanshaw commanding. Other pens, infinitely greater than mine, have already depicted the devastation in pretty little Belgium and beautiful France. But the sights from the car windows stirred great waves of pity across my heart, because some ten years before, practically in my boyhood, I had travelled these fair countries on a tour of military observation, and could appreciate how terrible and large had been the wounds inflicted.

Our particular camp was at Ploegsteert.

I have said that it was the reports of Belgian atrocities which mainly made the motive for the great outpouring of Australian manhood into the fray. We had heard these stories and believed them. On March 16, when we entered the village of St. Elois, I saw with my own eyes that these stories which had come to Australia were not lies. My first confrontation with the shocking facts was when in this village. We came upon a shattered convent. I cannot tell you its name because whatever inscription had been on the building was smashed in the general wreck. But the ancient archway of the entrance still stood, and on the heavy, iron-bound door was the " exhibit " in the case. It was the nude body of the Mother Superior. The villagers so identified her. She had been nailed to the door. She had been crucified. In the ruins we brought out the bodies of four nuns, unspeakably mutilated. Their bodies had been stabbed and slashed each more than one hundred times. They had gone to martyr-

THE BIG FIGHT

dom resisting incredible brutes. They had
fought hard, the blond hair of their assassins
clutched in their dead hands.

In this same village we found a white-
haired blacksmith—he must have been all of
seventy years—tied to his anvil. His hands
had been beaten to a pulp. They were held
together by a bayonet thrust through his
wrists. And on his anvil, weighted with a
horseshoe, was a note in German which
read :

" You will never shoe another horse be-
longing to our enemies."

I was shortly afterward to kill a German on
whom I found a letter evidently just written
and ready for mailing, wherein he told of
a score of atrocities in which he had par-
ticipated. He described the horrors as
" great sport."

One sprightly paragraph told of murdering
four women at St. Julien while carrying out
orders to loot all homes of every ornament and
article of practical device containing brass,
steel or copper. In this instance, as of others,
he said the looting had been " great sport," a
phrase he seemed very fond of. But quite
astonishingly his heart had been moved when

HUN BEASTLINESS

the four women, one of whom they shot and
the other three they bayoneted, had fallen on
their knees and begged for mercy. He wrote
that he was rather uneasy in his mind about
that, but at the same time said that he had
gathered from their home some very valuable
and interesting " souvenirs." Good God!
" Souvenirs! "

My first contact with the Germans was at
Wytschaete. I was given eighty men with
instructions to take the " skyline " trench
ahead. A skyline trench means just what it
says—the enemy trench on the horizon. It
was a night attack. It was a dangerous
trench. The Warwicks had three days before
taken it and then been blown to annihilation.
This sort of thing was constantly happening,
I was told. The British with bayonets could
rout any bunch of Germans out of any trench.
But at that time German artillery was far
superior. As a matter of fact at that time the
English batteries were given daily only six
shells for each gun and barrage fire was unknown. No British gun might fire a shell
without a particular objective view. There
could be no general storm of shells sent at any
suspected point.

THE BIG FIGHT

It was necessary for my commanders to know what was beyond that first-line trench, what there might be in machine-gun and "pill-box" emplacements, how strong a force might meet a general charge of our special contingent.

As a trained soldier I was therefore detailed to make this raid. No Man's Land at this junction of the fighting line was fully 500 yards wide.

The Germans had so effectually blasted all other attacks on the skyline trench, and our artillery had been so weak in its retorts that the enemy figured themselves secure. No star shells were glaring over No Man's Land as we made our way across. But we were cautious. It took us all of three hours, starting at midnight, before we came to the first line of enemy barbed wire. We nipped it down successfully, and still without discovery went through the second wire barrier.

But by this time the Germans were awake. They started everything they had at us in the way of rifle and machine-gun fire, but the only men of my company who hesitated were the ten who were shot down. We got at them with the bayonet, and they didn't like it.

In less than fifteen minutes we had turned them out of the trench. And the second trench.

Then I was to have my first encounter with the rottenness of German degeneracy. In the second trench captured we heard voices in a dug-out, and I called to know who were down there—how many.

The answer came up :

" Six German wounded."

I believed them.

I detailed Platoon Sergeant O'Harper to go into the trench and see what could be done for the wounded.

I got a shock right afterward. It was O'Harper's cry :

" The damned dogs have stabbed me ! "

So ten of us followed O'Harper into the dug-out and " cleaned up." There were nine Germans down there, and none of them had a scratch until we got at them.

I am afraid I ceased thinking of Germans as human beings from that time.

We didn't hold that trench very long. I don't think it was more than half an hour. Information regarding the attack had been sent back to the German artillery, and the two trenches we had captured were sent heaving into the air. My men were slaughtered all around me. But their sacrifice was not in vain, because I had been able to judge and estimate for the information of my commanders the lay-out and strength of that particular position. I had sent a messenger back with my report and rough sketches. I hoped to hold the trench until reinforcements might come at dawn. But it was useless for the rest of us (I was afterward to find out that only twenty-five were left of my original eighty) to remain in the face of certain death.

I ordered a retreat. German star shells were making day out of night in No Man's Land, so we got together and dug in about one hundred and fifty feet from the trench whence we had fled. We camouflaged ourselves with corpses only too readily at hand.

I sent back another messenger and secured reinforcements of three machine-gun companies and two hundred men. I hated the idea of giving up those two trenches.

When daylight came we were given another German "treat." Above the wreck of the skyline trench bayonets stuck up, and on them were the severed heads, with horrible smiles under their English caps, of twenty of my men.

When we saw that we all of us went into a blind rage. We swept across a narrow strip and charged the Germans right and left. They hate the bayonet. They will march shoulder to shoulder with astounding dogged-ness against the most withering fire. But the cold steel is not for Hans.

We drove them out in less than ten minutes. But they had other "things" to show us in those trenches as to the treatment put upon our men. We found four of our boys crucified to the doors of dug-outs, and we found others of our dead whose corpses had been horribly and obscenely outraged.

We had to give those trenches up. The Germans' big guns came after us within half an hour, and our own artillery had nothing with which to reply. But we stayed there long enough to take the heads of our boys off the bayonets, their bodies down from the doors and to give them burial as best we might. Also under a demoniac fire, stretcher-bearers took away a small, smashed soldier I had fallen over in a shell-hole at the

close approach to the German trench the
night before. When I fell over him he moved
and I grabbed him by the throat, not knowing whether he was friend or enemy. However, there was no resistance, and I instinctively felt that I had in my hands a weak and
wounded man. I let go his throat and he
gasped :

" Warwick ! "

He was only a little chap, scarcely twenty,
and was all broken up. He had a broken
arm, both legs had been broken and several
of his ribs. He had been caught in the fall of
a great upheaval of earth and stone shot forth
by one of the German two-hundred-pound
shells, but had managed to crawl out into the
air and wriggle his way to a shell-hole. In
this shell-hole he had lain for nearly four days.
His emergency ration had sustained him, but
he was mad with thirst and pitifully unnerved.
He threw his arm around my neck like a
child and begged me not to leave him. I gave
him drink. I had to lie to him, telling him
that I was going back to send for an ambulance when in reality I had to " carry on "
with my men. I left my emergency rations

with him. And I was particular to make a mental picture of the location of the shell-hole in which the boy had found shelter, and the following day was able to send him stretcher-bearers. You get a particular interest in such cases, and I am glad to be able to say this lad went safely to " Blighty " and lived.

CHAPTER X

TRAPPING SAPPERS

MY first big adventure in No Man's Land occurred at Ploegsteert in the Flanders campaign. I was sent out on patrol duty with five men in my command. For the war front it was a very quiet night. Guns were silent. Star-shells were absent. The enemy evidently didn't expect anything of us, nor we of them.

But what might be happening in that streak between enemy trenches that constituted No Man's Land was never a certainty to any commander on either side. They detailed me, therefore, to find out if the Germans were attempting to move in any way towards our position. I was to find out if there had been a movement or advance of any kind such as might be suggested by a line of trench newly thrown out.

In so far as the progress of my five men and myself were concerned it was easy going. We advanced well across the equator of No

Man's Land without detection and much farther.

It was, as a matter of fact, all too quiet. We had gone too far without detection as my judgment kept warning me. I was frankly afraid that we were walking into a trap. The Germans rarely left the dividing line of No Man's Land unguarded. To be sure, I had worked my men from our own trenches and through a land of stubble and hillocks. Most cautiously we had hidden from time to time in our advance to note if anything moved ahead.

No Man's Land in its aspect in this locality presented a hard problem for night observation, in that many small trees had been smashed by artillery fire, leaving stumps that an observer in the night might take to mean a sentry.

One such object appeared to me because of its absolute immobility to be surely a tree trunk. I am mighty glad I didn't jump at my first conclusion.

I told my men to "get down," which brought them prostrate to the ground. I ordered them to hold that position until I could find out what the strange figure in the night might mean.

THE BIG FIGHT

I crawled toward it, and crawled for at least twenty yards before I was positive that it was no shell-broken tree. I saw the man move. He was not moving watchfully but wearily. He had a bayoneted rifle in his hand, and as I moved toward him he stuck the bayonet point in the turf and leaned on the butt in the manner of a man thoroughly tired out.

It was all very silent in No Man's Land, and I had to move with extreme caution, particularly to avoid ruffling the gravel over the stones. There wasn't much shrubbery left which I might crackle in my advance. Such as was there was so dampened by rains and mud that you could pass over it without making a sound.

So I got to this man without his having the slightest suspicion of my approach. And it was the meanest job I had to perform of the war. Because, when I got to him I saw that he was really standing at the top of a tunnel. What this tunnel might mean I do not know. But, of course, I knew that it led somewhere, and that at the end of it this single soldier would have reinforcements.

Other men who had gone over No Man's

TRAPPING SAPPERS

Land before me had given information which guided me in this situation. Such sapper tunnels had been frequently made in No Man's Land by the Germans to meet and defeat British patrols. The usual thing had been if you saw a man standing in No Man's Land to shoot at him. He was supposed to be wary enough to detect your advance, and, while jumping down into his tunnel protection, to let go a discharge of his rifle which was a signal to the other end of the tunnel of an enemy patrol approach. At this other end from twelve to eighteen men would be stationed. The single man at one end of the tunnel was merely bait to betray the scout patrol into firing at him. At which the Germans would send half of their force through the tunnel to support their single sentry while the other half at the other end of the excavation would take to the surface, speed along and come on top of the discovered entrance to the tunnel. In this wise they would have the enemy patrol surrounded.

I had never been in one of these engagements before, but I had been thoroughly well instructed as to what you must look out for. This sentry would have been a simple mark

for a revolver shot. He did not know that I
was there. He stood at ease, a perfect target.
But the report of a pistol shot would have been
as perfectly a report to his comrades of our
presence.

To get him, as I have learned in America
to say, "right," my duty was to knife him.
I got up behind him all undetected. I never
felt such miserable hesitation or qualms of
conscience in my life. I had lost all revulsion
at destroying human life when it was German
human life, because I had already seen that
they rather took an insane joy in killing their
fellow man. But to sneak up behind one and
stab him to death was a very difficult thing to
do. I had to bring into my mind the reason
and cause for my act. There were dead men
right behind me in No Man's Land to create
a moral support.

And when I felt this I did get up and without hesitation stabbed him in the back of the
neck. I stabbed him in the neck so that he
might not be able to make outcry.

Then I went back to my small force of
men. With the Germans at the other end of
the tunnel thus left unsuspecting the advantage was all with us. I sent three men to

follow the line of this tunnel, and immediately on sight of the enemy give attack, while I led my other two men through the tunnel from the entrance where I had slain the sentry. So thus we had reversed the expected. When my men "on top" gave the attack and the German patrol sought retreat into their tunnel, we met them with quick revolver firing and bombs. And we killed all but one. But he was shot six times and had no chance to live. I'll grant him he was brave. We set him up with such first-aid articles as we had, and then I tried to pump him as to the position behind. He wouldn't tell. He smiled at me and thanked me for having his wounds bandaged. But he was a square and nervy patriot and wouldn't talk at all. I did not attempt the persuasion of telling him that his life could be saved nor did I attempt to prevail upon such gratefulness as he may have felt for our attention to him. Not but what I hated him; not but what I detested him as the type of which I had sworn to myself deserved no mercy. Yet the man died with a steady loyal look in his eyes; and you cannot help but respect that.

The discovery of this night was of extreme

value in that it informed my officers of the higher command of a German engineering plan to undermine our position.

From the sentry I killed and from two others of the men killed we possessed ourselves of papers of interest to my superiors. And also from the lieutenant killed who was in command of this squad in No Man's Land I took documents which I will herewith reproduce in the belief that the reader may find particular interest in a German official document designed to instruct their own men against the dangers of the gas attack, which they began and out of which pure necessity caused us to retaliate. These papers had their value to the British commanders by way of guidance in future gas attacks.

Here are the instructions accurately translated :

H. Q. 6th Army   *Army Headquarters.*
1V B. No. 19388   **26**   **7**   **15**

To the subordinate formations (including Technical Services down to battalions and detachments inclusive).

Appendices 1-3

The C. G. L. of the Field Army has issued the following under his number 3582 R, 3803 R.

TRAPPING SAPPERS

dated 18. 7. 15 viz. " Instructions in case of a Hostile Gas Attack " and " Notes on the Protective Measures to be taken to meet a Gas Attack " drawn up by the 2nd Foot Artillery Brigade and the 4th Army, and based upon actual experience in combating hostile gas attacks.

(Sgd.)   Von Hartz.

Appendix 1

H. Q. 4th Army   *Army H. Q. Thielt*
1 a No. 1/28   28   6   15

From all parts of the Army suggestions have been submitted to Army H. Q. for weakening the force or even entirely neutralising the effects of a hostile gas attack, apart from the use of respirators and oxygen breathing apparatus. These suggestions show what trouble the commanders of all ranks have taken to advise means of protection for our troops against the effects of the enemy's gas. Many of the suggested devices are theoretically practical. In many cases actual experiments have given successful results. Nevertheless, none of these devices can be employed, for the simple reason that before they can take effect the enemy's gas has reached our troops. Further, the employment of such devices is *not necessary*. The combined fire of our Artillery, Infantry, Machine Guns, Minenwerfer and Hand Grenades breaks up the gas clouds, and the respirators then afford complete protection against such gas as may reach our position.

The aim and object of all training in combating

*gas attacks must be to instil into the troops complete
confidence in the fact that our fire and the respirators
afford complete protection against the effects of gas.*
The possession of this confidence by every man
is the surest guarantee that, in the event of a
hostile' gas attack, he will remain calmly at his
post, allowing the gas cloud to pass over him.

The following Notes have been drawn up in accord-
ance with this view and should be issued to all
Officers and Men. The Notes lay down the lines
upon which the systematic training of the troops
is to be carried out. The system of training and
the scheme of actual defence are briefly described
below. I request all commanders to exercise a
constant supervision over this training and to use
every means in their power to attain the object
described above.

INSTRUCTIONS FOR COMBATING HOSTILE GAS
ATTACKS

(1) All troops in the trenches must be fully
equipped with respirators; the respirators must
always be kept in such a condition that they are
ready for immediate use. Officers and Medical
Officers must, by frequent inspections, satisfy
themselves as to the above.

(2) It is not desirable that the men should retain
their respirators when in rest billets. When
troops are going to rest billets, respirators will be
withdrawn from them, preferably under Company
arrangements; during the period of rest they will
be examined and stored by the Medical personnel

and re-issued just before the men return to the trenches.

(3) In order that the respirators may be always ready for use small quantities of anti-gas solution and water will be kept in readiness by the Medical personnel in front line for the purpose of re-moistening the respirators.

(4) Machine gunners, artillery observers and, when possible, all officers in the front line will be issued with oxygen breathing apparatus (*Selbstretter*). It is desirable that men who are used to working with the apparatus in peace time should be de-tailed to assist artillery observers and machine gunners in the use of the apparatus, to enable the latter to carry out their particular duties undis-turbed. Special stress·is laid on the necessity for affording every possible protection to the machine gunners and artillery observers.

(5) The Pulmotors and large oxygen apparatus must be kept in readiness at suitable points behind the front—the situation of all this apparatus should be known to the troops.

(6) As soon as the weather conditions favour a hostile gas attack, all commanders must exercise the utmost vigilance. All the above-mentioned protective appliances will be once more inspected as regards numbers and conditions. In par-ticular all preparations should be completed so that, the moment a gas cloud appears, fire may be opened by Artillery, Infantry, Machine Guns, Minenwerfer and Hand Grenades. At the same time care should be taken that the equa-

nimity of troops is not disturbed by all these preparations.

(7) At the first sure sign of an impending gas attack a signal will be given for donning respirators and opening fire. It is specially desirable to direct enfilade fire on the area covered by the gas.

(8) It is a mistake, before or at the beginning of a gas attack, to leave only a weak garrison in the front trenches and withdraw the remainder of the troops into the support trenches, as the effect of the gas will be equally felt in these. It is almost equally mistaken, to allow the men to withdraw laterally along the front trench. It is imperatively necessary that every man should remain in his place and commence firing.

INSTRUCTIONS FOR TRAINING IN COMBATING HOSTILE GAS ATTACKS

(1) *Training to be directed by Officers.*

(1) Instructions as to the harmless nature of a gas attack if a timely and correct use be made of the respirators, and if a combined fire of all arms be directed against the gas cloud.

(2) Drill in putting on the respirators, fire being opened immediately afterward.

(3) Respirators to be worn while firing.

(4) Instructions regarding wind and weather conditions which favour or prevent a hostile gas attack.

(2) *Training to be given by Medical Officers.*

(1) The use of the respirator.

(2) The rapid improvisation of a substitute in

case the respirator has been lost or become unserviceable.

(3) Training of Officers, Artillery Observers, Machine Gunners, and a number of other suitable men in the manipulation of the oxygen breathing apparatus. Special stress is to be laid on the training of Artillery Observers.

(4) Action to be taken by a man who has inhaled gas or whose eyes are suffering from its effects.

(*Sgd.*) Herzog Albrecht von Wurtemburg.

Appendix 1*A*

Headquarters VI Army.
1*V B No.* 19388.

Notes

(1) A hostile gas attack is only possible when the wind is blowing toward our trenches and then only in cloudy weather or darkness. A gas attack cannot be carried out when the wind is blowing in the other direction.

(2) None need fear a gas attack. The fire of our artillery (which in its retired position remains unaffected) with the combined fire of our infantry, machine guns and hand grenades, breaks up the clouds and prevents the enemy from following it up. Further the respirator affords complete protection, it should therefore be put on immediately a gas cloud appears, and fire should be opened against the latter.

(3) The gas cloud can approach with great rapidity, therefore the respirator should be rapidly and

correctly adjusted. Every man must learn by repeated practice to adjust his respirator quickly.

(4) The respirators must always be kept in perfect order, they are only effective when damp; the anti-gas solution can be obtained from Medical personnel. Every man is responsible that his respirator is ready for use.

(5) When the gas cloud appears, it is imperative that every man remain in his place and not take shelter in dug-outs and not withdraw to a flank or to the rear.

(6) In case the respirator is lost or becomes unserviceable a substitute should be extemporised immediately, a cloth containing damp earth or a damp cloth should be firmly pressed on nose and mouth. A makeshift respirator is better than none.

(7) Should any man inhale the gas the Medical Officers have apparatus ready at the dressing stations which at once banish the ill effects.

(8) Gas does not injure the eyes, at the most it causes temporary irritation.

Appendix 2

H. Q. 2nd Foot Artillery Brigade
No. 4 B 430 Secret

INSTRUCTIONS IN THE CASE OF A HOSTILE GAS ATTACK

In the case of a hostile gas attack, in addition to opening the heaviest possible fire, the main effort must be directed toward preventing the gas cloud from reaching our lines, or at any rate breaking it up to such an extent that it is harmless. This result is best obtained by creating upward currents of air which are most easily produced by means of highly inflammable material placed close in front of our position. The most suitable materials for this purpose are hay, straw, old sacks, wood shavings, etc., soaked in paraffin, etc., so that they can be readily ignited even in wet weather.

On the approach of the gas cloud the fire must be lighted by some reliable means of ignition. According to a statement of a prisoner the French intend to combat the gas cloud by the ignition of black powder.

Appendix 3

H. Q. 2nd Foot Artillery Brigade .
B No. 430 15 *Secret*

Notes on the protective Measures to be taken in case of a gas attack.

1 PREPARATIONS.

(1) Heaps of inflammable materials soaked with paraffin should be placed, if possible, at several points in front of the position.

(2) A supply of the above materials should be kept stored in the shelters, so that the fire can be kept burning for about half an hour.

(3) Every man should be supplied with special matches or other means of ignition which can be relied on in a wind.

THE BIG FIGHT

(4) Respirators must always be kept ready for use.

(5) All oxygen apparatus must be maintained in a serviceable condition (individuals who are equipped with such apparatus should be exercised in its use).

ACTION TO BE TAKEN ON THE APPROACH OF A GAS CLOUD

(1) A heavy fire should be opened with guns, machine-guns and rifles against the source of the gas cloud.

(2) The fires should be lighted all along the front and kept burning.

(3) The respirators should be firmly placed over nose and mouth as soon as the gas penetrates the position.

(4) Breathing should only take place through the moistened respirator.

(5) The gas cloud should be fanned upward by means of waterproof cloths (ten squares).

CHAPTER XI

SPOTTING

I was to be a lucky man in that there were few branches of the war in which I did not have experience until a German bomb laid me low at Bapaume. I not only got an opportunity to do my country service in the air as a military observer, though it sent me on my first trip to a hospital, but not so very long afterward had the wildest and possibly more thrilling experience in command of one of His Majesty's ground " dreadnoughts," the famous tanks.

Mind you, I wouldn't paint myself as so brilliant and indispensable generally that the aviation corps was trying to steal me from the infantry, and the special tank service from doing duty in the air.

But it is to be recalled that I was a trained soldier—that I had had ten years of study and practice of military affairs. I must credit myself with always having been ambitious. And so, when war came, I had several strings to my bow that must surely prove of value. One of these was the acquirement of an expert knowledge of wireless telegraphy and telegraphy generally. I had also picked up a considerable knowledge of photography. And, naturally, I knew gunnery. There was a dearth of men in the British air service at the time competent for an observer's duty, scarcely more than half enough to man the hundreds of aeroplanes that were being turned out under forced pressure. For the battle of the Somme was now under preparation and it was not only desirable but imperative that Britain's aviators should take the mastery of the air. Scores of other young officers like myself, possessing special qualifications for the work, were requisitioned from the other branches of the army and put into intensive training as aviation observers.

The tragedies of Gallipoli and Belgium I had been through had not impaired me in any degree. Shell-shock had not shattered my nerves; physically I was in the best of shape, and tests of my vision met all requirements.

You can wager though that I said several prayers during my practice flights. Once you got up in the air, however, there would come

over you an amazing confidence in the trust-
worthiness of the fragile planes and the roaring
motor.

The darts, loops, banks, and volplaning
that had at first turned me somewhat dizzy, I
found myself getting used to. And there's
another thing about flying. It's when you
get 'way up. The farther up you go, the less
you think about falling. Or if you do, the
vastness of the upper regions simply takes all
thoughts of self-importance out of a man.
You are such a midget in the immensity after
all. And you find yourself figuring, "Well,
suppose I do drop? What a small thing I am
anyway in this great world." And it sets you
thinking of the millions of men who have died
in the great cause and to wondering why you
should imagine you must of necessity be one
of the lucky ones to escape. Flying would
even take the "swank" out of the Kaiser or
his booby-faced son.

For all that, however, there was one time
in every flight when I held my breath—when
I never quite got over being scared. That was
the landing. The observation machine we
had, while not so fast as some of the fighting
flyers, was nevertheless capable of about one

hundred miles an hour. When you are going at that pace you swallow a lot of wind whenever you attempt to talk or, rather, shout. In machines of that speed, as the reader probably knows, they begin to drop as soon as the pace goes under sixty miles an hour. That means you have to make your landing at a whooping, whizzing speed, and if you are forced to a landing away from your station and on rough ground, there will usually be bruises in the adventure for you at least. Lord bless me! But the earth would suddenly seem to be coming up at you fast—at express-train speed. Even the flyer will admit to you that it is the hardest, most nerve-racking feature of his nervy job. Just when you bring the wheels of the machine on a level with the ground there must be a swift upward turn—it is a ticklish proceeding, requiring " feel " as much as scientific knowledge of the levers, and if you don't do the thing rightly, your plane will balk viciously, jabbing its nose into the ground, rearing, probably somersaulting, possibly smashing itself, and you too.

I soon came to have absolute confidence in my flyer, however. He was Lieut. Reggie Larkin, and of my Gallipoli comrades, the

Australians. He is now a youngster of not much more than twenty years. But he had soon shown in training the peculiar faculties, which are as much artistic and psychological as scientific, for the making of a fine flyer. He was always superbly confident of himself when he took to the air, a confidence that was contagious and of great aid to a novice like myself. And of his bravery I have a stirring account to give before this chapter closes.

As for me, after the first two or three training flights, I had not much time to think of myself. I had to make a showing in acquiring the use of the set cinema camera with its purpose of acquiring continuous bird's-eye views of the enemy's positions, and in mastering the working of aerial guns and the new problems which they presented. This included the study of plaster models of landscapes, with special reference to promontories, the better to judge altitudes and for gun-aiming at what lay below your sweeping aeroplane.

Now I come to my most thrilling aerial adventure—my trip through hell in the clouds, a battle with a whirling Fokker, at that time Germany's crack fighting plane, of gaining what we went out and up after, and of the superb courage of Lieut. Reggie Larkin in guiding the machine through a tempest of attack, though his face was ripped and bleeding because of shrapnel wounds.

On the line between Albert and Orvilles there was an especially vicious, strong battery. It had done deadly and ferocious work on our trenches. It was the more dangerous in that it evidently possessed a perfect camouflage of natural foliage. Several attempts that had been made to spot it had failed. One of our observation planes had been smashed by the " archies " and its crew killed in the attempt to discover the exact location of this battery.

On a morning when the battery had developed an especially deadly activity Larkin and I were sent up to hunt it. We made rapidly into the air above our own sector, soon reaching an altitude of 20,000 feet. Before descending over the enemy's territory we thought best to investigate the upper regions to see if the Boche had any of his own men up with the plan of performing their favourite method of attack at this time. This would be done by the speedy Fokkers, who would take high altitude, and, hidden behind the clouds, occasionally dart forth into the clear, looking for victims. Were such discerned, the Fokker would come plunging down upon its prey, letting go everything it had in the way of gunfire, and frequently blasting the objective aeroplane into a total wreck. This is the method that the young American crack, Lufberry, has used with havoc on the Germans. He carries three guns, two that shoot through the propeller, and one over his head.

If there was any pouncing of this character to be done, Larkin and I had decided that we would take a shot at the trick ourselves, but first, of course, with the consideration of escaping detection altogether if we could, for our most important task was to send back the knowledge of the location of the big, murderous battery.

The upward tendency of sound is almost as powerful as telegraphy. You can actually hear the chirping of birds at an altitude of more than 1,000 feet. But when your own motor and propeller are humming and throbbing into your ears it is hard, if not impossible, to hear the other fellow's.

Evidently the enemy's observation balloons had spotted us for all our efforts at hiding behind the clouds at the dizzy altitude of 20,000 feet, and had given the alarm. Suddenly a Fokker came cutting through the mist not more than fifty yards away from us. I looked to see others come soaring at us, and was convinced there were probably machines below ready to trap us should we seek flight by descent, as it would be likely for us to do from such a great altitude. But at any rate only our single enemy was in sight.

There wasn't an instant wasted by either of us in manœuvring. We had come to such close quarters there wasn't much chance. There was only one flyer in the Fokker, and he let go at us with his machine-guns the second he saw us. But in spite of his promptness I appeared to have beat him to the fire. Or perhaps it was at the very same time we got at it. How on earth such a storm of splitting bullets were sent at me without my being hit is still a matter of wonderment to me.

His bullets did tear through one of our wings and it was turned and crippled slightly, but not enough to bring us down. Larkin manœuvred swiftly above the Fokker, and I knew what for—it was a chance for me to use my bombs. I let four go at the German in as many seconds.

SPOTTING

They did the work. We saw the Boche's Fokker stagger, could make out the smashing of its engine in a sheet of flame, saw the complete blowing away of one of the enemy's wings, and if the pilot himself was not blown to pieces then and there he must surely have been killed a few minutes later, for the Fokker went plunging to earth like a dead thing, and, later, when we came out of the clouds ourselves to take observations for the location of the battery, we saw the wreck of the aeroplane near an enemy trench. It was reduced to a mere heap.

I thought, right after we got the German, that our own time had come. For our aeroplane began falling with a rapidity to make one gasp for breath. It was describing the most eccentric spirals and plunging almost as dizzily as the Fokker. I yelled at Lieut. Larkin, though hopelessly, my voice sounded so small. I was dazed. Yet he told me afterward that my voice reached him. It caused him to turn his head. For the first time I saw his bloody, wounded face. I saw also that his hands had fallen away from the controls, and that he was reaching out helplessly toward them.

THE BIG FIGHT

Of course, when we came into sight out of the clouds the enemy had started all the "archies," and shrapnel from a bursting shell had torn Larkin's face cruelly. The shock had knocked him out for a brief instant. I admit having uttered a swift, frantic prayer as I saw him reaching out so feebly to regain his controls.

But with his splendid courage he suddenly braced. We were about 1,700 feet above the enemy lines when he again succeeded in taking direction of the machine. To have tried to climb directly up again in the enemy fire must have meant our destruction. We would have been too fair a target. Instead, Larkin boldly shot straight downward directly toward the aerial batteries and the trenches. They thought us hit and falling, and fled from their places in fear of being caught in the crash.

Larkin shot his plane not fifty feet above the Boche trenches, but none of the occupants took even so much as a rifle shot at us. They either ran or cowered in the trenches as we swept past. Then he shot up again, cleared a small, wooded section of knolls, and dropped behind them, thus successfully getting out of the range of the "archies."

SPOTTING

Larkin turned once again to me his blood-reddened countenance. This time he grinned bravely, coolly.

"It's quite all right, Dave," he called. "The wounds are nothing. I'm feeling quite fit again. We've got to spot that battery."

So up we went. We mounted some 15,000 feet. The "archies" promptly and furiously got after us again. They spread a circular fire about us. That is the way the "archies" go after aeroplanes, not shooting directly at them but trying to surround them with a fire that must smash them whichever direction they may take in seeking to escape destruction.

Meanwhile, I was working my camera for all it was worth, and peering upon and around the country with my glasses. There were several small clutters of heavily wooded knolls marking the landscape below us, and the rattle and roar of the "archies" were suddenly joined by the crash and boom of bigger guns and the distant reply of our own batteries.

I began banging my wireless exultantly. For down in the largest clutter of knolls, under a cloak of foliage so naturally dense and perhaps artificially assisted, and affording full concealment ordinarily, I had seen those in-

THE BIG FIGHT

stant sudden sparks or flares as emitted from the throats of the big battery's guns in action.

Additionally, I dropped red lights, visible in daylight, over the battery's position, which was hardly necessary, for my wireless was working perfectly, and I was soon giving our guns the enemy's range.

But the first fire from our side was poor, and I was therefore excited and indignant.

"What the devil's the matter with you?" I wirelessed, repeating the instructions. "If you can't do better than that I'll have to get the infantry to teach you how to shoot!"

I chuckled to think how the artillerymen would like that.

It was enough to make them try a shot at us.

But a minute later a shell ripped right through the trees that camouflaged the battery, tearing a big gash in the concealment.

"Bull's eye!" I shot out into the air from my key. "Give'm hell!"

With that Larkin started us for home, with the "archies" spitting their rage but ineffectually.

But just the same something did happen that made all a blackness for me until I woke up in a hospital clearing-station just behind our lines.

Brave old Larkin was the cause. He had held his nerve and strength, and never did he falter until we were home and within twenty feet of the ground, when he suddenly lurched forward and was " out." We crashed to the ground, and I also was " out."

There wasn't much the matter with me. I was only pea-green from bruises for a week. But Larkin, poor chap, had two ribs and a leg broken in addition to having suffered the shrapnel wounds on his face.

CHAPTER XII

"RAZZLE DAZZLE"

It was at Beaumont Hamel, about September 16th, that I got my chance to command a "tank."

The dear girl was named "Razzle Dazzle." She was very young, having been in service only three months, but rather portly. Matter of fact, she weighed something over thirty tons. And in no way could you call the dear little woman pretty. She was a pallid grey and mud-splashed when I got her, and there was no grace in the bulging curves of her steel shape. Or of her conical top. Or her ponderous wheels.

The fact is that she showed every aspect of being a bad, scrappy old dearie. The minute I saw her in her lovely ugliness I knew she would like trouble and lots of it. Her metabolism was a marvel. She carried a six-hundred-horse-power motor. And out of her grey steel hoods protruded eight guns. An infernal old girl, you can bet she was. All ready to make battle in large quantities.

When I boarded " Razzle Dazzle " she was full of dents. She had rocked around among several trench charges. But the reason for my assignment to her was prosaic. Her captain had not been killed. He was just sick—some stomach complaint. I was drafted on an hour's notice of the job, this because of long training in handling rapid-fire guns.

It was all new to me, but highly interesting. My crew consisted of seven men—five of them well experienced. And a black cat. Although she was a lady-cat she had been named " Joffre," and I can't tell you why because I never received any explanation on this point myself. But " Joffre " was very friendly, and insisted on sitting either on my knee or shoulder from the moment I sealed myself and my men in the tank. We had our outlook from several periscopes above the turret and from spy holes in the turret itself.

The order had come to me about one in the morning, and it was nearly three when we started lumbering out toward the enemy trenches. We had about six hundred yards to cover. I knew little or nothing of her motor power or speed. My concern was with the efficiency of the guns. She bumped and swayed across No Man's Land at about four miles an hour. She groaned and tossed a great deal. And, in fact, made such poor progress that my regiment, the Oxford and Bucks, beat the old dearie to the enemy lines. Our men were among the barbed wire of the first line, fighting it, cutting it, knocking it down, before the old " Razzle Dazzle " got into action.

But she " carried on " just the same. And when she smote the barbed wire obstacles, she murdered them. She crushed those barriers to what looked like messes of steel spaghetti.

Instead of sinking into trenches, as I feared she would, she crushed them and continued to move forward. Of course, we were letting go everything we had, and from my observation hole I could see the Germans didn't like it. They had put up something of a stand against the infantry. But against the tank they were quick to make their farewells. It was a still, black night, but under the star-shells we could see them scurrying out of our way.

This was very sensible of them, because we were certainly making a clean sweep of everything in sight and had the earth ahead throwing up chocolate showers of spray as if the ground we rode was an angry sea of mud.

Every man in the tank was shouting and yelling with the excitement of the thing, and we were tossed up against each other like loosened peas in a pod. Only " Joffre " remained perfectly cool. Somehow she maintained a firm seat on my swaying shoulder, and as I glanced around to peer at her she was calmly licking a paw and then daintily wiped her face.

Suddenly out of a very clever camouflage of tree branches and shrubbery a German machine-gun emplacement was revealed. The bullets stormed and rattled upon the tank. But they did themselves a bad turn by revealing their whereabouts, for we made straight for the camouflage and went over that battery of machine-guns, crunching its concrete foundation as if it were chalk.

Then we turned about and from our new position put the Germans under an enfilade fire that we kept up until every evidence was at hand that the Oxford and Bucks and supporting battalions were holding the trenches.

But this was only preliminary work cut out for the tank to do. I had special instructions and a main objective. This was a sugar refinery. It was a one-storied building of brick and wood with a tiled roof. It had been established as a sugar refinery by the Germans before the war, and when this occasion arose blossomed as a fortress with a gun aimed out of every window.

To allow it to remain standing in hostile hands would mean that the trenches we had won could be constantly battered. Its removal was most desirable. To send infantry against it would have involved huge losses in life. The tank was deemed the right weapon.

It was.

And largely because "Razzle Dazzle" took matters into her own hands. The truth is, she ran away.

We rocked and ploughed out of the trenches and went swaying toward the refinery. I ordered the round-top to be sealed. And we beat the refinery to the attack with our guns. But they had seen us coming, and every window facing our way developed a working gun. There were about sixteen such windows. They all blazed at us.

My notion had been to circle the "sugar mill" with "Razzle Dazzle" and shoot it up from all sides. We were getting frightfully rapped by the enemy fire, but there was apparently nothing heavy enough to split the skin of the wild, old girl. Our own fire was effective. We knocked out all the windows, and the red-tiled roof was sagging. As I say, my notion was to circle the " mill, " and I gave orders accordingly. But the " Razzle Dazzle's " chauffeur looked at me in distress.

" The steering gear's off, sir," said he.

" Stop her, then, and we'll let them have it from here," I ordered.

He made several frantic motions with the mechanism, and said :

" I can't stop her either."

And the " Razzle Dazzle " carried out her own idea of attack. She banged head on into the " mill." She went right through a wide doorway, making splinters of the door, she knocked against concrete pillars, supports, and walls, smashing everything in her way, and bowled out of the other side just as the roof crashed and smothered all the artillerymen beneath it.

On the way through, the big, powerful old girl bucked and rocked and reared until we men and the black cat inside her were thrown

THE BIG FIGHT

again and again into a jumble, the cat scratching us like a devil in her frenzy of fear.

Closed up in the tank as we were, we could
hear the roar and crash of the falling "mill,"
and from my observation port-hole I could
see that it was most complete. The place
had been reduced to a mere heap. Not a shot
came out of it at us.

But still the "Razzle Dazzle" was having
her own way. Her motorist was signalling
me that he had no control of her. This was
cheerful intelligence, because right ahead was
a huge shell crater. She might slide into it
and climb up the other side and out. I hoped
so. But she didn't. She hit the bottom of
the pit, tried to push her way up and out,
fell back, panted, pushed up again, fell back,
and then stuck at the bottom of the well,
throbbing and moaning, and maybe penitent
for her recklessness.

Penitence wasn't to do her any good. It
wasn't five minutes later when the Germans
had the range of her and began smashing us
with big shells. I ordered my men to abandon
her, and led them in a rush out of the crater
and into small shell-holes until the storm of
fire was past.

"RAZZLE DAZZLE"

When it was, "Razzle Dazzle" was a wreck. She was cracked, distorted, and shapeless. But the runaway engine was still plainly to be heard throbbing. Finally a last big shell sailed into the doughty tank, and there was a loud bang and a flare. Her oil reservoir shot up in an enormous blaze.

"Razzle Dazzle" was no more. But she had accounted for the "refinery." And our infantry had done the rest. The German position was ours.

I was all enthusiasm for fighting tanks. But my superiors squelched it. For when I asked for command of a sister of "Razzle Dazzle" next day a cold-eyed aide said to me :

"One tank, worth ten thousand pounds, is as much as any bally young officer may expect to be given to destroy during his lifetime. Good afternoon."

He never gave me a chance to explain that it was "Razzle Dazzle's" own fault, how she had taken things into her own wilful control. But he did try to give me credit for what "Razzle Dazzle" had herself accomplished. He said the destruction of the "sugar mill" had been "fine work."

THE BIG FIGHT

I wonder what " Joffre " thought of it all. I don't remember seeing her when we fled from the tank, except as something incredibly swift and black flashed past my eyes as we thrust up the lid. I sincerely hope she is alive and well " somewhere in France."

CHAPTER XIII

MOUQUET FARM

THE name of Mouquet Farm flashes vividly to my memory a night of the bitterest, bloodiest fighting I ever went through. It certainly was the hell of war in its most intensive degree. There were twenty-two hours of continuous fighting with never a minute's let-up in the gales of deadly missiles.

We were holding Orvilles in preparation for the great battle of the Somme, and our immediate objective was Thiepval. This Mouquet Farm, with its powerful batteries, presented a particular obstacle, for it was directly in our path on the road to Thiepval. It had to be obliterated. But before we might move on Mouquet we must dispose of a skyline trench just ahead. The farm lay three miles to the right of this skyline trench as we faced it.

If we could battle through those lines to Mouquet Farm and capture or put into retreat the batteries that had been constantly and effectively in use against us, it would mean that we would make the whole German position untenable and place ourselves in a position of great advantage in preparation for the great Somme drive.

We were over the top at ten o'clock one night from our own elaborately constructed trenches. My regiment, the Oxford and Bucks, had been living in " Fifth Avenue." I had the hardest task keeping my own two platoons in leash. From eight o'clock that night they had known they were going over the top, and after the usual ceremonies of letter-writing to the dear ones at home they got so restive I could hardly hold them in the trenches. They hadn't been in action for nearly a month, and this hadn't pleased them. The very mildest-dispositioned of my men were actually bloodthirsty for a crack at the Germans. The recollection of the barbarities that had been visited on their comrades killed and injured in Flanders, their realisation that the Germans had abandoned themselves to absolute mercilessness and brutality in warfare, had the opposite effect the German policy of " terrorism " hoped to achieve—that is, to break down the *moral* of

our men. It made our men all the hotter and
eager to meet the enemy, and it nerved men
who had an inherent abhorrence of man-
killing not only to go through with the nasty
work, but to go to it furiously. Finally the
call came for the men to file before the ser-
geants and get their " tot " of rum, and everyone, of course, knew what this solemn little
ceremony of the trenches meant.

Armed with a revolver, a couple of bombs,
and my short-armed bayonet, I led my men
over, and we had a front position in the advance. Ahead of us our big guns poured a
powerful barrage fire. But the enemy was
sending back a tremendous reply. We had
seven hundred yards or more to traverse to get
to Hans, and his guns swept us destructively
every step of the way. The knowledge of our
advance got to him quickly enough, and the
night fairly went aburst with light in a flood of
star-shells. In their high, ghastly glare I saw
scores in the ranks of our advancing men
scattered and sent reeling by the bursting of
the shells; I saw whole regiments caught by
the accuracy of the German fire and battered
frightfully. But there never was a pause in
the advance. The lines would get together

again, the advance would consolidate anew, and we would " carry on."

My own little group got along splendidly. There was but a single tragedy among us. It was sufficiently terrible, but almost miraculously it cost the life of only one man. He was a bomb-bearer. He was carrying a box of the explosives for use at close range when we actually came upon the German trenches. A piece of shrapnel struck the box. There was immediately a deafening roar which pierced through the grand noise of the battle, and the poor fellow was blown utterly to pieces. Fragments of his body were whipped into the faces of his comrades. The whole platoon halted and were shaken for an instant, but at a yell from me got their nerves back with admirable promptitude and threw themselves along in the advance.

Then our front lines walked into a drive of rifle-bullets and bombs and we made our first rush for the Germans. The star-shells suddenly disappeared. Out of the glare in which we had been advancing, in an instant we found ourselves fighting in inky darkness. Hans had no intention of illuminating his barbed-wire barriers to aid us in the irksome

task of cutting them down and clearing them
away. But our barrage fire, we were soon to
know, had done some very good work in this
direction. Most of the barbed-wire barricades
had been obliterated by the rush of our heavy
shells.

The work of routing the Boche out of that
sky-line trench was very swiftly done. We
gave them bombs a-plenty, and then smashed
right down into the trench and its traverses
after them with knife and pistol and more
bombs. We cornered group after group of
them in the " bays."

As I climbed across one of the trench
parapets I nearly fell over a man's leg. I
leaned forward to feel for a supposed enemy,
grasped the leg, seeking to pull the man forward. To my horror I stood with a severed
leg clutched in my hand.

And a tremulous voice came up, the tone
indicating a mere boy :

" Norfolk, sir," he said. " I'm terribly
wounded. For God's sake don't leave
me."

Three days before the Norfolks had made
an attempt to take this trench and had been
all but entirely wiped out.

THE BIG FIGHT

I found both the lad's legs had been carried off by a shell; but he had torn his shirt to strips and saved his life by making tourniquets for his severed limbs. But he had lost his water-bottle and his emergency rations, and had been suffering horribly in his place of concealment in the parapet. How he had remained undiscovered there by the Germans for three days is a marvel, save that, of course, he was concealed from sight in the parapet and it had been his good fortune that no German had been sent to take station in that particular spot.

It would have been more fortunate for the poor lad if he had died at once. For after all his agony he was to die on the stretcher that was bearing him back to the field hospital on our first line.

We did take eight prisoners whom we found huddled in a bay. But these were wounded men. They were Bavarians. They told me there had been great dissatisfaction among them against the merciless rigours of discipline and cruelty practised by their officers, that several times outbreaks had been imminent, but a stern order had been posted threatening instant death to one out of every twenty of them to be picked indiscriminately for slaughter at the first signs of revolt.

We had no time to consolidate the trench and its traverses, and hold against a counter-attack, for the Germans were back at us with reinforcements, the worst feature of which was a preponderance of machine-guns. We had no chance of standing successfully against it, so I ordered my men out and into No Man's Land. For a while it looked as if they were going to smash us all the way back to our own lines. They sent up their star-shells only fitfully, and as we crawled and stumbled back into No Man's Land I thought for a moment all was over with us indeed, thought we had been cut off and surrounded. For out of the darkness came the rush of scores of men. They almost carried us off our feet.

" Who's there? " I demanded, but not expecting anything but a bomb for my trouble.

To my great relief, though, the response came :

" Anzacs ! "

" Oxford and Bucks ! " I yelled back joyfully. " Who's commanding? "

" Lieutenant Foster. For God's sake, is that you, Dave Fallon? "

THE BIG FIGHT

"Foster of Sydney!" I cried earnestly. For Foster had been one of my pupils at the Royal Military School of New South Wales— a splendid young chap and one of my most intimate friends.

We groped our way to each other in the darkness and fairly hugged each other.

"Fancy!" said Foster, "meeting in this hell-hole!"

The sweep of fire was growing more intense, more deadly. A dozen of our men were dropped. We decided to hold on together.

The German fire was ceaseless, the shells for ever showering, the "minnie" shells cutting straight over our heads with a concert of noise that nearly arose to a scream. Our own artillery roared and thundered its reply, but we had no way of observing its results.

Why the Germans didn't realise their advantage and sweep over No Man's Land and annihilate us I don't know. I'm only too grateful they apparently didn't think of it, or, thinking of it, misjudged our strength. I know Foster and I expected every minute they would come rushing out after us. And in this predicament came a new source of worry. It was now past four o'clock in the morning. My men had experienced no sleep for many hours, and the work of keeping up a barricade had driven both them and the Anzacs to the point of absolute exhaustion. With every sort of explosion smashing and crashing around us, danger and death on every side, yet the men would throw themselves prone on the ground and drop off into sleep as if a bullet had brought them the deeper sleep of death itself. Foster and I and our N.C.O.s nearly dropped ourselves at the exhaustion of the task of keeping them on their feet. Besides, we had constantly to give aid to our wounded. My best orderly, Price, had uttered a cry behind me, and I turned to find him with his right leg blown off. I applied a tourniquet, and Price is now somewhere safe in Blighty. Twenty of my men were killed outright during the night. As many Anzacs, if not more, died.

At intervals in the night I had sent back messages to our lines describing how imperative reinforcements were, but for hours no reply came to us, and I could not but think that in bullet-and-shrapnel-swept No Man's Land every one of these messengers had fallen. As a matter of fact, two were killed. But two others made our base, and one of these came staggering back to me before dawn, his forehead gashed by shrapnel, but with cheering words that help was soon to come. I bandaged the plucky man's wound, thanked him warmly for his good service, and then—my turn came.

Right over us a shell burst. I was whirled around, thrown, staggered to my feet, only to be helplessly tossed again to the ground. This time I got up more slowly, crawled to my knees, and stood swaying, when two of my men gave me quick support.

There was a stinging and burning sensation in my right shoulder, with every second or two swift pangs of pain. My coat had been half ripped off my back. I sat down, leaning against three dead men, while Foster of the Anzacs and a sergeant bared my wounds and examined them under electric hand torches. Partly embedded in the torn flesh they found a shoulder buckle of my coat and removed it. And then and there also they managed to extract the largest of the pieces of shrapnel that had struck me—the nose of an explosive shell cap and a slug of steel that was found, on subsequent examination, to be one and a half inches long and a quarter of an inch in diameter. This had scraped my shoulder blade and was protruding from the fleshy portion of the arm. Afterward five smaller pieces of shrapnel were to be removed from the wound.

But Foster and the sergeant made a wonderful job of treating the wound with iodine and binding it, so that within fifteen minutes such weakness as had seized me passed away, and although the wound hurt and my arm hung numb and useless at my side, I could continue my duties and was able to hang on for many hours more, able to carry the fight back to the sky-line trench when reinforcements came, and have the satisfaction of knowing that we were firmly established there and that an expedition of considerable strength was on its way to give battle for the Mouquet Farm position. It was a week later, while I was in a hospital, I got news that the farm was in our hands.

A sharp, overwhelming attack had been delivered in which a battery of French seventy-fives, brought up and concealed in a quarry, aided the infantry, with a big band of English and French aviators as well, who swooped right down over the Germans, delivering tornadoes of machine-gun fire, and scared them into complete flight and to the desertion of some of their heaviest guns.

But that's getting somewhat ahead of my story. At five o'clock that morning reinforcements came to Foster's Anzacs and my thinned-out platoons in the form of the Huntingdon Cyclists regiment and two companies of Engineers. You may be sure the Huntingdons weren't riding their bicycles over No Man's Land, but had been impressed as infantry for this affair. The German fire never let up, but the Engineers blasted temporary trenches for us in No Man's Land, and the Huntingdons had brought with them an extra number of machine-guns. A steadily moving train of bearers was arriving with sandbags for the strengthening of our position.

Thus with the coming of dawn we faced the German trench not more than one hundred yards away on something like even terms. And soon we were topside in advantage, for our shells began to find the German dug-outs and smash down the barbed-wire defences the enemy had renewed in the night. By noon we were back in the German trench from which we had been driven. And reports from other battalions all along the line began to tell of similar successes in the attack. By noon the entire German position had been taken. There were two fierce counter-attacks and a weak one. Then with the arrival of further reinforcements we started in pursuit of Hans, and he fled in panic to the Mouquet Farm protection.

I did not want to leave the fight, and stuck several hours after Col. Reynolds, my commandant, had sent me word that I was to return, and that Capt. Reed, of A Company, would be along to relieve my battered platoons.

By eight o'clock that night, however, my shoulder wounds became angry with pain, and I was weak and chilled. I received word through a messenger that Capt. Reed was within ten minutes of arrival. So I dropped exhausted into the seat of a field ambulance beside its driver, the body of the car being crowded with more dangerously wounded men. At Orvilles I switched to another ambulance and was able again to sit with the driver. In this I was whisked to a field hospital located in the captured "Hohenzollern Redoubt," now well behind our foremost lines. There the other pieces of shrapnel were removed from

my shoulder, the wound thoroughly cleansed
and professionally bandaged.

All this time I never really thought of myself as being out of the fight, and had full
intention to return, but the doctors ordered me
to Wimereux (a charming seashore resort it
had been in peace days), and I remember meeting a professor of English in an Egyptian
college whom I had met while we were training
for Gallipoli, who waved to me as I sat beside
the ambulance driver with my arm in fresh
white bandages and a sling. I learned afterward he had arrived in France only the day
before, and had been immediately ordered into
action.

" Lucky beggar, you Fallon," he shouted
laughingly to me, and indicated my arm.
" What wouldn't I give for that Blighty ! "

He was killed in the Mouquet action the
very next day, and of the five officers of the
companies which relieved mine four were
killed. I had been indeed a very lucky man.

Via Gazincourt and Boulogne I made my
way to Wimereux, where I was assigned to
the Hôtel Splendide, which ha been trans-
formed into a great hospital. For a month I
had a perfect rest, rambling the sea cliffs, read-

ing, catching up with my correspondence with old friends, playing with the pretty little French kiddies on the sands, and staring out on the restful sea, where, however, as a reminder of war, there was an island on which Napoleon in the long ago had constructed a fort and naval base for his contemplated invasion of England.

My wound gave me little or no trouble, healing nicely from the start, and in a month I was ready to return to service.

While I was at the Splendide, Capt. P. A. Hall, M.C., sent me the information that I had been officially recommended to headquarters for " capturing sky-line trench, consolidating and holding it during heavy, continuous shell-fire, and rendering first aid to the injured until hit and relieved."

CHAPTER XIV

SPIES

THE thoroughness with which Germany in her plotting to conquer Europe, and later the world, had infested every country with spies, the Americas as well as Europe, had organised a system spreading to the antipodes, has been written history for some time.

There is no doubt that they managed at the beginning of the war to honeycomb the armies of their opponents with these "informants"—Germany doesn't like the designation "spies."

Well, in the first place, I can attest to the deftness with which they tapped our telephone wires between the sectors of battle-fronts. But I can also attest that while German scientific ingenuity was sharp and clever, the German mind was frequently childlike. For we led them into many traps. German thoroughness of preparation, German patience, German sheep-like concert of action—these must be granted. But subsequent events of the

SPIES

war showed that whenever Joffre, French, Pétain, Haig, Byng, the Grand Duke Nicholas ever faced the greatest of the Boche generals with anything like an arm of equal military strength, the Boche was beaten. Serbia, Roumania, Belgium, the child-sized nations of the world—these have been the conquests of the would-be international bully. Noble laurels surely and properly fit to adorn the low, brutal, thick-fleshed brow above the pig-eyes of a criminal empire!

But to get back to spies.

The Oxford and Bucks was enjoying a rest, encamped near the little, shell-wrecked village of St. Elois in Belgium. Our most welcome visitor for several days was a young peasant girl, decidedly attractive because of raven hair and very blue eyes. She brought us the Continental *Mail*, she served us with home newspapers, she sometimes brought us roast fowl and other homelike edibles to enhance our soldier food. She was frequently, as well, entrusted with our letters for mailing. She had a smattering of English, which was the first unusual thing I noticed about her. Peasant girls of the locality can always make a stagger at French, frequently enough know a little

German. But I had never met one before who could turn a word in English.

About this time the accuracy with which the Germans were planting shells along the roads of our Very rest camp became remarkable, also how neatly they seemed to be able to time their shots and how accurately along the roads which the supply wagons travelled toward the front lines. If it had been guesswork it would have been uncanny, and none of us for a minute believed it to be guesswork.

One evening a private of my platoon came to me with the information that he had happened upon the girl seated in a small dug-out in one of our trenches most intently studying a paper spread upon the top of the basket in which she usually brought the edibles she sold us in camp. This private had the good sense to saunter along as though he had observed nothing. I warned him to continue to say nothing and went looking for the girl.

She had still an armful of newspapers to dispose of, and I observed her in her free passage in our lines, joking with our soldiers, smiling, affable, and, you would say, the most simple-minded and innocent of maidens.

She never asked questions, but she would

frequently stand over men at play with cards and watch the game apparently intently. But, at other times, if you watched her you would find her standing near a group of our men who might be discussing our own immediate affairs —our position, what they had learned or guessed of their commanders' plans. Every one had a pat on the cheek and a smile for Marie.

It did not seem possible there could be any harm in her! I began to think that the private had seen her poring only over some scrap of newspaper or periodical she had found, most probably one that had on it a photograph or drawing that engaged her attention. He admitted he didn't get a good look at it, but also insisted he was quite sure it was a piece of writing or pencil drawing.

However, as Americans say, it is "bad business" to dismiss such matters in war with a wave of the hand. I decided to follow the girl. She strolled easily down the road to St. Elois in the twilight. I held off the road behind her as much as I could—wherever the brush would give me footing. The road was nearly if not quite deserted at the time. A few peasants' carts passed. And I noticed that only one of these peasants apparently knew Marie. They all·nodded to her, but they nod to any stranger on the road in that country. But one spoke to her, stopped his horse, and they conversed for a minute or more. The talk began with smiles and banter, but presently it seemed to take on a more serious turn. Finally he nodded his head in very decided confirmation of whatever he had told her, started his horse, and she resumed her journey to St. Elois. But she no longer strolled. She moved with a smartness of step that kept me going briskly in the concealment of the bushes and trees beside the road to keep up with her.

Marie halted before a half-smashed house. The roof was gone and the upper walls, revealing in stark desolation the empty chambers of the upper storey. But the ground floor of the house remained intact. Marie loitered for several minutes at this house before she entered it. In fact, she waited until darkness had completely enveloped the place. I stole up to the house and groped around the walls. In the rear a light popped out of a window.

I wasn't by any means certain that these

things meant Marie was a spy. For all I knew she might be a refugee. One found many a refugee Belgian family quartered in such battered places in those days. The fact that some of the peasant carters had apparently not known her could also be laid to the same circumstance—that of her being a peasant girl who had fled from a village in German possession.

But simultaneously with the popping up of the light I heard a sound that swept from my mind all such explanations regarding Marie. It came quite clearly—the cooing of pigeons. That, decidedly, I didn't like. The carrier-pigeon has played an equal, if not greater, part with any other method of secret communication. Not one of the great Powers of the war but has from 100,000 to 125,000 such feathered informants working between their headquarters and stations in the enemy lines established by spies. The wireless, telephones, secret codes, expert signalling of modern warfare have not supplanted the carrier-pigeon.

He had proven his usefulness in war long ago—in the Franco-Prussian war. It was at the time when Paris was cut off from the rest of the world that fanciers in the French capital

went to the authorities and explained that if
the birds were sent to Tours by balloons they
would return with whatever news was entrusted to them.   Accordingly, more than
eight hundred homing pigeons sailed as cap-
tives out over the fortifications and as certainly returned with information—so much
and in such detail that Parisians have since declared that put into book form it would have
made at least five hundred volumes.

By a process of micro-photography the
equivalent of a sixteen-page newspaper was
reproduced on a film which was inserted in a
quill and fastened to the middle tail feather
of the bird.   These films were thrown on a
screen through a lantern that magnified them,
just as moving picture films are now shown.

Belgium from that date took the training
of these birds, and it was from this little
country that most of them were purchased,
and there they had been most largely bred at
the outbreak of the war, and Belgian trainers
have been busy in the training of them ever
since for the Allies.

Through the lighted window I saw the girl
in closest conversation with a man of peasant
type.   They were going over a small bundle of

papers on a roughly hewn table with the lamp between them. There was just the rudest furnishing for habitation in the room that had been the kitchen of the house. They were so interested in the papers that it was obvious the opportunity was as good as any I could expect to take them by surprise. So I stole away from the window and to the back door of the house, which opened directly into this room.

I managed to open the door without alarming them, but was so intently keeping my eyes on them as I crept into the room that I stumbled over a loose brick in the floor of the shell-shaken house. Man and girl leaped to their feet. He lost no time reaching under his blouse for a pistol. But here I had him clearly at a disadvantage. My own automatic was already in my hand. I shot him straight between the eyes.

The girl shrieked and started toward me in fury. She had no weapon, so I thrust my revolver into my holster and grappled with her. She fought vixenishly for a few minutes, but then suddenly relaxed in my arms and began violently sobbing. After that she very quietly accompanied me to battalion headquarters. Once over her fit of fury, she made no pretence that she had been other than a spy in our camp. But she said the man had compelled her to do this work. She was a native of Belgium, but of mixed Flemish and German parentage. She said the man was a German; she had known him to be all the while, but said she loved him, and that it was only her love that had persuaded her to act as informant for him. Now that he was dead, she said she did not care what became of her, what punishment was given her.

"You can kill me too. I didn't like to do the things I did when the men in your camp were always so friendly and kind to me," she said, "but I would do anything my man asked me to. He could make me do anything."

From the dead man's pockets I secured many papers, going to show that he had for a long time had accurate knowledge of the locations of our railroad crossings and stations, the times of the movements of our convoys and the paths they took, the times of relief in our trenches.

The girl led me to a cote camouflaged in the shattered roof of the house where were more than a dozen homing pigeons. I took her then to battalion headquarters. Later, at her trial, her life was spared, but she was sentenced to twenty years' imprisonment.

On several of the transports which brought the original 20,000 Australians to Egypt for training were detected more than a dozen spies. One was caught red-handed tampering with the boiler of one of the transports. A ship's officer came upon him and there was never a word exchanged between them. The officer sent five bullets crashing into the spy's head, blowing the top of his head off. Two other spies were suspected, watched, caught and shot. But several others escaped who tampered with the machinery of the ships to an extent that caused great delay and in one instance at least necessitated the return of a convoy ship to an Australian port for repairs.

At St. Julien I had also direct knowledge of the workings and capture of a spy—a clever one he was. As at St. Elois, the Germans seemed possessed of a wizard knowledge of our position, and their guns were regularly popping their shells into places within our lines which we regarded as most well-concealed.

But from the church tower of the smashed village behind us watchful men one night saw the eccentric whirling and flashing of a mere pin-point of light. The village was deemed to have been surely scoured of spies. In fact, most of the inhabitants had been ordered away from the place because at that time spies were so thick, and Belgians and French, supposedly, so often turned out to be of German antecedents or even of German birth, that the commanders had been all but ruthless in sending the people away.

But none had suspected the padre—a small, gentle-voiced little man. I had often seen him and bowed to him. Good Lord, come to think of it, I had often commiserated him on the misfortune of the loss of his entire flock!

An officer and a dozen men, the instant the information was reported of the flashing tower light, were dispatched to the church. They met the good little padre serenely stepping out of its portal. He was asked if there was any method of access to the tower. He smiled deprecatingly.

" It is no more than a false tower—a poor ornament on a poor church. There was never a place for a bell in it," he answered. " Nobody, gentlemen, could gain access to that tower but a monkey or," he laughed in a quiet way, " an aeroplane, and the good English seem to have driven all the Boche aeroplanes away."

" But the light flashing in the steeple, Padre?" insisted the British officer.

" There are little coloured panes of glass in the tower," he answered readily enough, " put there to be of ornament when the light of sunrise and sunset should rest upon them. Might not the flares of your guns have flashed reflections from the panes? "

The officer considered. He said to me afterward that he was quite convinced of the padre's honesty, but thought that German spies might have made their way by rope ladders or some other fashion to the tower. He declared that it was more by force of habit than design that he asked the " padre " to remain until he and two of his men had investigated the matter.

They weren't long in finding out that the " padre " was a liar. They found a firm spiral iron stairway leading up into the tower, and within commodious quarters where there were a heliograph, rockets and flash lamps of various sizes.

Meanwhile the "padre" was telling the soldiers that he would go down the road a little way to his modest home and there await the officer. And the unsuspecting soldiers were about to accede to the request, when the captain and his men returned from their investigations.

The "padre" suddenly produced a pistol and it spat its fire twice in the darkness, wounding one soldier, but before he could fire again the soldier nearest jabbed him in the throat with his bayonet. We were to learn afterward that the real padre of the church had accompanied his flock in its exodus, and though we never learned anything of our "padre," it is certain, of course, he was no priest but an enemy spy.

In the trenches before the battle of Mouquet Farm we got the news of the capture and death of one of the boldest of spies that ever operated among us. This man had been for days familiarly about the trenches in the uniform of a British artillery officer. His English was as faultless as his manner was affable and his monocle firm in his eye. I have never learned what led to his detection, but I witnessed his arrest and saw him ten minutes later led to execution—a brave man, I must confess, able to smile philosophically in the face of death and wearing his monocle as debonairly as ever.

I have been asked so often whether in the excursions that I made from time to time into the German lines in quest of information, had I been captured would it have meant a spy's death before a firing squad? So I suppose the public generally does not understand the difference in classification between a scout and a spy. As a scout, I went forward to the German trenches wearing my British uniform. If caught, I was entitled to treatment as a prisoner of war. Were I to wear a German uniform and suffer capture, then the assumption would bring upon me a spy's death. This is according to the agreements laid down by the Hague Convention. Germany, however, has proven itself so utterly incapable of " playing cricket " in the game of civilisation and mankind, that I am heartily glad they never caught me at my scouting tasks.

CHAPTER XV

IF you should ask me what feature of warfare was harder and fiercer than going " over
the top " in the lot of an infantryman, there
would be no hesitation about my reply—
" Wood-fighting." Some of the most deadly
contests of the war have been held in the
woodlands of the battlefields.

And the worst of it was, the British soldier
was all but an absolute novice at the game.
There was lack of suitable training grounds in
England, and we had no time for training and
preparation once we got into France. We
had to go right into this dangerous character
of fighting. Its peculiar perils make constant
call on the wit and cunning of the individual
fighter.

This last is the chief necessity of this particular game; it is invariably a duel of wits
between individual fighters. Each unit concerned has to win its own little fight. It
cannot, as a rule, expect help from its own

troops on its flanks. For these cannot see to fire at the foe of the especially beleaguered unit. Besides, if they seek to come to the aid of another unit, they cannot see because of the trees and shrubbery what they themselves may be leaving unguarded. Nor can an attacked force rely on the support and reserve coming up quickly. It's slow moving in the woods.

Besides, your aeroplanes cannot inform your commanders of the size of the force they are going up against or much of the manner of its arrangement. The foliage hides this knowledge. And in no other fighting is it so necessary for the " little officer," the commander of a small unit, to be self-reliant. He is thrown entirely on his own resources and must win his own fight unaided. Unceasing caution must be the watchword. And the soldier in this fashion of fighting is useless who has not the ability to fire instantly and accurately on a suddenly appearing target.

My own first experience at the game was in the attack on Delville Wood at the great battle of the Somme. I was then a platoon commander with sixty men under my command. At this time artillery fire was not so scientifically carried out as it was later so marvellously to be. But our "heavies" were supposed to have destroyed the wire entanglements and the machine-gun emplacements to be encountered in our advance.

When the signal came for the attack on Delville Wood I sent my men out and into it promptly. But I had already dispatched two scouts to find out, if possible, if the wire entanglements on the first enemy position had been smashed by our guns. One of them soon signalled back that the wires had been untouched by the artillery fire, but that he and his companion were at work cutting them down. That was not a job to be left to only two men, and I ordered an advance of my platoon in fours. When we got to the wire it was to find both of my scouts dead—one with a bullet straight between the eyes, the other had been struck in the heart.

The sight of them fired my men to determined effort to get past the wire. But we had to stand an appalling fire as we worked. Five were killed outright, six put out of the battle by serious injuries. The fire not only came from an enemy we could not see behind the trees but from snipers up in the trees and hidden in bushes. The wire itself was crowded with bomb traps. And there came also the drum fire of machine-guns and the hail of shrapnel.

Then I thought the last hour of all of us was at hand. For as we now advanced, each man practically for himself, but also aligned about abreast, the ground gave way under us. An old German trench had been carefully and most deceivingly covered by a treacherous intertwining of branches and foliage with an under layer of barbed wire, and we were plunged, struggling and kicking, into what looked like a hopeless trap.

The Germans thought surely they had us. The enemy rushed out from concealment with bombs and trench-knives and rifles. If we had remained there we would surely have been slaughtered. I yelled at the top of my voice encouragement to my men. And they answered with plucky cries that they would follow me.

How we got out of that trap I don't know, but out we came, every man of us, in spite of the fire that swept us. Our hands and faces were torn and bleeding from the barbed wire, our clothing ripped to shreds. But these splendid men of mine took the fight straight

THE BIG FIGHT

at the Boches. It was just plain hand-to-hand fighting—trench-knife clashing against trench-knife, revolvers and rifles blazing directly into one another's faces.

My gratitude can never abate toward that little company of superbly brave men I led in Delville Wood that day. For time and again they drew around to protect me. They recognised that the Boches were seeking to make a special mark of me. For a long time British officers had given up the practice of going into action in uniforms bearing the special insignia of their rank. The only indication of that now is on the identification tab that hangs on an officer's neck. But, of course, at such close quarters, the Germans readily observed that I was in command, and their instructions are always emphatic on that point—" Kill officers first."

A big fellow named Morrison—in spite of the confusion of the fight I swiftly, sharply noted the spectacle—had actually gone wild with rage. He attacked a huge Boche with tremendous fury and literally hacked the man to pieces with his trench-knife.

And when his enemy went down, Morrison turned with a terrible leer on his countenance, made crimson by spurting blood from a big gash in his forehead.

" There, sir," he yelled exultantly, " there's a fine piece of German sausage for you ! "

The Germans turned tail and we carried on through the wood, keeping in touch with the platoons on our right and left by means of " piles," that is, men set out at certain intervals to find out the positions of the people on our flanks so that we might not be surrounded and cut off from the main body.

Our artillery in the meantime was sending out its heavy stuff and shrapnel well ahead of us, trying to cut off reinforcements for the Germans.

Our objective we knew to be a knoll of considerable height and length some two hundred and fifty yards through the wood from the scene of our first encounter. The Australians had tried to capture the wood two weeks before and were rent, torn, and sent reeling back when they had edged their way through the forest to this knoll. For on it the Germans had built a strong position of sunken concrete houses thoroughly equipped with field artillery and machine-guns. And their

M   187

axes had effected a clearing in the woods surrounding this position. An attacking contingent was therefore forced into the open
before their guns.

Sent back in defeat, the Australians were
nevertheless able to bring knowledge to the
heavy batteries of the location of this dangerous hill which was really the commanding
position of the entire Delville Wood. So
while we were advancing, the big guns had
been giving the hill the merry devil, but
without destructive effect. Still, they had
blown shell craters all about the position, and
these craters were to give us the opportunity
for some shelter in our advance in the open
and for the setting up of our machine-guns.

The question became, however, after we
had put the first group of Germans on the
run, as to whether there were other forces
intermediately placed to give us opposition in
our advance on the fortified hill.

One of our airmen tried to get us the information. He came down within less than
five hundred feet of the tree tops. The growth
was dense, but he signalled that for as much
as he could see there was nothing in our way.
He had no sooner given the information than

a chunk of shrapnel blasted his engine, and the sorely wounded plane swerved, keeled over, and crashed through the trees and down to our side-lines. Our aviator was but little hurt, the trees having broken his fall, and we anxiously questioned him as to our flank forces for we could not know whether they were also keeping up the advance.

There were some two hundred and sixty of us who finally came out from behind the trees to make the effort to carry the hill. A great burst of fire greeted us. But it didn't stop us. We went up the knoll, scrambling for a foothold, digging footholds for ourselves with trench knives and trench tools. Yet the way was steep and we came reeling down again in a swish of bullets and great, choking showers of earth. Six times we tried to take that little hill. Small reinforcements heartened us in the last two attempts. It was a splendid struggle by stout-hearted men.

But at last the orders came for us to move back, and again our heavy batteries began to smash at the hill in the hope of bringing the forts to destruction, the enemy into confusion, and thus to give us something like a good chance at the foe. This attempt went on for half an hour. While the artillery did some damage, yet when its attack ended the Germans were still there among the little, sunken concrete forts on the hill crest with a force of infantry below in the hollow ground.

We began all over again the bitter, bloody struggle. Out we advanced from the shelter of the wood to endure the fiery abomination. And this time we " got there " ! Even now I do not know just how we gained success where before we had failed.

There was the enemy still on the slope, still protected in his concrete forts, and with machine-guns and bombs at hand. And the snipers were working with sickening accuracy from tree tops and ground concealments, potting us through clearances in the foliage especially prepared to make us their open targets.

But our boys worked their way forward with a wonderful sort of deliberateness, fighting their way upward on the knoll in small packs. In some marvellous fashion enough of us survived—I think we must have numbered five to six hundred in this final successful attack—to swarm about the German block-houses, smash our way inside, strike, kill, and finally so terrorise the Bavarian defenders that they completely surrendered. In the larger block-houses there were companies of about forty men. In the smaller, groups numbering about fifteen. From these garrisons we took some four hundred prisoners.

The prisoners told us that they had deemed the attacking force a much larger one than it really was, but they had not dared retire—had stuck and fought so desperately because they were ordered to defend the position to the death and feared to retire to the main body because of the punishment they felt sure would be meted out to them there.

There were other features of that advance through Delville Wood than the final, ghastly drive up the armed hill. Deadly perils they were and which we continued to run into in the four days following as we grimly, under frightful shell fire and many counter-attacks, held on to the ridge. Escaping the barbed-wire entanglements, there were the dangers of hidden pits dug by the Germans. At the bottom of these pits were bayonets rooted so that their points came uppermost, and as we marched along we would go plunging head foremost into these pits, falling on the points of the bayonets. Under other camouflage of foliage were concealed the deadliest mines. Did you step lightly on them or stub them with your toe they would blow you to pieces. Rifles were cunningly wrought into the barbed-wire entanglements in a manner to be unseen. Contact with the wire electrically set the rifles blazing at you from all angles with almost the certainty of their bullets killing at least one or two of the wirecutters.

It wasn't to be supposed that the Germans were going to let us sit peacefully down to our tea and jam in our hard-won concrete forts. We had no sooner got the wounded started on their way to the field hospitals, and sent the surly four hundred prisoners trudging back to our main lines under guard, than the first counter-attack was made. We drove it off. They tried three times again that day, but were smashed back every time. They kept us hopping all the time—nearly every hour for the four days we held the ridge—under their shell fire, but their artillery did not do much more execution to the position than had our own.

When they couldn't get us out that way

they tried gas. This was the worst horror, for many of our boys in the advance through the woods had lost their gas helmets. These had been torn away from their equipment by tall bushes or the low-hanging branches of trees. It is horrible enough to see a man struck down by a bullet or shrapnel or bombed to pieces. But the gas victim is most piteously horrible of all. Only too many of our boys got this gas, and it was harrowing to see them writhing in agony.

We had not found the taking of Delville Wood impossible. But nearly so. We had strength and determination, and by this time in the war a bitter hatred against the barbarians we knew to be guilty of such countless atrocities, against an enemy who doesn't know the means of fighting fair. Yet the victory had been very, very costly in lives—too terribly costly. Of my original sixty men I brought back only fifteen.

The casualties were so numerous as to change subsequent military plans for taking a wood. We try now to outflank it, to cut the wood off from the other lines of communication. The heavy artillery sweeps the woods, trying to destroy the strong emplacements.

Then we go on either flank and try and cut it off that way.

Since Delville Wood and Gonnecourt Wood, which were similar actions and just as murderous and bloody, it has been calculated that by direct attack the cost is all too great. Incidentally in that action I was a very lucky man. Two bullets went through the skirt of my tunic and I had four bullet or shrapnel dents in my helmet. I think, as a matter of fact, they were all bullet dents from snipers in the trees.

The handling of men in a wood fight is in all ways difficult. Men go plunging into unseen dangers through over-zealousness. If the enemy runs away continue to fire at him, but do not chase him—follow him cautiously. The possible traps are too many for headlong pursuit.

I lost only too many good fighting men that way. For when they saw the Germans they dashed after them, became separated, were trapped. It is hard to keep men together when advancing through a wood. The ideal method of moving in such environment is a long, straight line, moving steadily forward and not in a series of disjointed ripples. When small hostile bodies are thus met they are easily driven back. If large bodies are encountered the whole line halts, keeping up a straight assault. If the first line is not filled up the part of it that is engaged will be reinforced by the sections in the rear of it, closing up with it. If this does not dislodge the enemy the units in reserve will be thrown in at the critical point.

When the company is held up by the enemy every man actually engaged must at once dig something in the way of protection. for himself with his entrenching tools. The support from the reserves do likewise, so that they may act as a rallying point if the company is driven back by a superior counter-attack.

However, I would not become technical with my reader. I would rather recall for him the deeds of fine courage done during wood-fighting.

Why, I saw one man alone take a strongly emplaced machine-gun station of the enemy. He was not so large a man but just full of rage and full of fight. He killed two men with bullets, a third with the bayonet, and scared the others into flight. Then he turned their own gun on the fleeing Germans and destroyed them to a man.

The British soldier is heroic in defending his officers. They are splendidly loyal. Once, when advancing through Delville Wood, a German sniper dropped out of a tree just behind me and would have riven my body with his bayonet, for I was utterly taken by surprise and had no chance to turn and defend myself. But one of my men struck the German on the head with the butt of his gun, splintering his skull.

I have seen men willingly sacrifice themselves to save their comrades. One threw himself on a German bomb that had dropped at my very feet. He took the full blast of the pieces, saving not only myself but many other men nearby. I saw, more than once, brave soldiers rush up to a fuming bomb and nip away the fuse within a second of the time the bomb must otherwise have exploded.

This lucky life of mine was spared remarkably on another occasion. As I was rushing toward the German trenches a Boche let go a bomb at me. It hit the stump of a tree. The stump got the full force of the explosion. With my revolver I got that particular Boche.

"WOOD-FIGHTING"

But I tell you there is hardly a day when I am not thankful for having seen in this war the heroisms and sacrifices of which my fellow man is capable. It is splendid to have had an opportunity to move in the ranks of these aristocrats of human bravery.

They took us out of the hell-hole in Delville Wood after we had stood the deadly gaff for four days, sending up a much larger relief force.

The pitiful remnant of my platoon, in common with the others returning, were in unbroken spirits. They turned from the tragedy of the knoll and marched out of the same woods into which they had forced their way against most frightful perils, singing, dancing, and skylarking, and we officers let them do as they pleased.

But I could not feel so happy for I knew that as soon as I got to my rest billet it would be my duty to write letters to the parents, brothers, sisters, relatives or nearest friends of my all-too-many dead.

CHAPTER XVI

THE PLAY SIDE OF WAR

THERE has to be a play side. Human nerves could not stand the strain of this modern warfare without some chance to alternate the light and frivolous with the tragedy of the struggle. It is not only that all war and no play would make the soldier a dull boy, but the fact is it would finish him up in short order. Every general recognises this. It is not a matter of sentiment. It is a matter of business—the business of war. Men cannot absolutely be made into machines, and they cannot work well in the grim business of war if they fall below a certain point in mental cheerfulness. Yes, men must be cheerful to fight well. Generals found that out long ago, and they acted on this knowledge during every day of the frightful conflict in Europe.

Not only were the men taken out of the trenches after a certain number of hours to "rest" them, to get them away from the noise and strain of battle, but also to give them a chance to laugh, to romp, to exercise all such diversions as the men's mentality may specially select. The chance to get emotional relief as well as physical relief, of which they all stand in need after the ordeal of imminently facing death, must be afforded them.

In "Restville" good commanders give their men opportunities of all kinds to ease their minds and bodies of nervous strain. Dancing, singing, sheer frolicking is smiled upon by the officers. Every sort of diversion is encouraged. Farmer soldiers and gardeners are supplied with materials with which to plant and tend little gardens. Other men are given facilities with which to sew or knit, artistic men are furnished with pencils, paper, charcoal, canvases and paints. Others put in their time composing songs and drilling choruses. In "Restville" there have also been fashioned beautiful statuettes in wood, striking models in clay.

Concerts and dramatic entertainments are common occurrences. There is always a great deal of fun obtained from the necessity of men assuming women's parts in these comedies. The work of preparing for such entertainment is often very elaborate.

THE BIG FIGHT

Nothing is too much trouble that has enough fun in it. And you may be sure that the audiences at these shows, which are sometimes held in the wreck of a theatre of a smashed French town or in a barn, or again in a dugout possibly 100 feet under ground, are rapturously appreciative. There are always many recalls. But the actors receive no reverence. They are yelled at by name and "kidded" extravagantly.

In "Restville" are foot races, steeplechases, catch-the-ring-on-the-bayonet races, dashes with gas masks, all manner of obstacle races invented on the spur of the moment.

The "catch-the-ring" may be taken as a good example of the ingenuity in inventing games having a relation to the war game itself. The race begins with a dash and ends with a difficulty. The difficulty is presented by a series of small rings fixed in posts along the course. Each man in the race reaches for these rings and must pass the bayonet through them with a single stab. The winner, of course, is he who successfully pierces with a single motion the most rings.

Airmen fly over "Restville," doing some of their fancy stunts for the amusement of the men below. Cavalrymen give exhibitions of hippodrome riding. Dances are encouraged in the hotels of these "Restvilles."

But whether in "Restville" or in action, one cannot help but pay a tribute to the cheerfulness of the British soldier. Tommy sings, laughs and jokes when marching along the white, dusty road in France even though he be dead fagged with the heaviness of his equipment. As the reinforcements move over the devastated territory and while shells fall all around him Tommy will sing, "Are we downhearted?" "Are we fed up?" The reply will come : "*NO! NO! NO!*"

During the suspense of waiting in the dug-outs and trenches and when the German heavies are sending forth a continuous hurricane of high explosives and shrapnel, and those born to die on the battlefield are being blown to pieces, the others can be heard singing, "I wouldn't leave my little wooden hut for you," "Mother Machree," "Home, sweet home," "Tipperary," and "Pack up your troubles in your old kit bag."

They—the men in "Restville"—talk a great deal among themselves regarding the wounds they wouldn't mind getting. Some would not mind a nice little " Blighty " in the arm, others express preference to a " Blighty " in the leg, and others, more careless, say that any old " Blighty " would do. They all have a common opinion, and that is that they would rather be blown to pieces than be blinded, gassed, or taken prisoner.

When going over the top in the face of murderous fire from shells and machine-guns one often hears some cheerful soul shout : " Keep in step ! Left, right, left ! I had a good job and I left ! " Or in the crowding as they start away, you will sometimes hear a man call merrily, " Keep your distance, Bill ; I'm not your little bit of fluff." This because of the natural tendency of men to huddle under such circumstances. It is a tendency an officer must combat, since men in mass can be pulverised by machine-gun fire, and bomb and shell explosions.

When a man falls someone is sure to say, " Poor old boy !—his day's work is done."

Or, again, in passing the wounded, the characteristic cry is : " Cheer up, I'll soon be joining you." Another kindly call to a wounded comrade is : " Keep a place for me in the next bed in hospital." I've heard the

Tommies running through German trenches, throwing bombs to the tune of, "You made me what I am to-day; I hope you're satisfied."

I can't think of how such spirits can ever be beaten. The *moral* of the British Army can never be destroyed.

And I desire to say right here that as for the German he fights like a dog under a master's lash. I have never seen a smile or a grin on a Hun's face, and never heard humorous remarks from his lips, and I have an army school certificate which asserts that I can understand German.

Even when the Huns are taken prisoners they bring all their surliness with them. After some heavy fighting on the Ancre, where we unavoidably captured a few Huns and sustained many losses, I ordered four Germans to carry one of my men who had been dangerously wounded. They refused, saying, "They would not carry the English dog." However, I punched them into obedience.

Once I had as a prisoner a German officer. One of my men felt sorry for him in his appearance of complete dejection. He went over to the man, and by way of commiseration offered him a cigarette. The German officer growled, leaped to his feet, knocked the cigarette from the Tommy's hand, and spat in his face. I never saw a quicker bayonet thrust in all my life.

As for the play side of war, who can ever forget the men of the East Surrey Regiment who on the Fourth of July, 1916, went over the top in the face of blasts of shrapnel, dribbling a football?

The Huns called those boys " Madmen." But our prisoners frequently admitted their admiration of that particular " stunt."

It is an everyday occurrence " over there " to witness a football match on some recently regained, devastated French field. Often enough shells from a German battery engaged in its usual afternoon work of strafing will be falling within a few hundred feet of the players.

I once acted as referee at a brigade boxing tournament when during the final bout Boche airplanes spotted us. They sent down bombs and darts, but we went on with our sport until a bomb fell close to the ringside and killed several spectators. Even then the crowd seemed bent on remaining to witness the end of the bout, until the brigadier commandant, one of the spectators, suddenly said : "We are a lot of damn' fools to stay here," and he ordered the bugler to sound the safety call.

Regimental, brigade, and divisional concerts are daily affairs in "Restville." Every company has its singers, dancers and jokers.

It may not strike you as a delicate or charming phase of trench sport, but in the summer months "Cootee-hunting" is the principal diversion. In other words, flea picking. These vermin are more terrible than the Germans in provoking our boys to profanity. Whether on the march, in the trenches or in billets, cootee-hunting is played by everybody from general to private. One trench game is to bet on who can capture the most cootees in a given time.

A pack of cards is a precious possession, especially in the trenches. The best known games for which they are used are Poker, Banker and Broker, Brag, Twenty-one, Crown and Anchor, and House.

The playing of these games provides a very necessary relaxation.

One day's picture of life in the trenches will convey an idea of its generality. You would find men not on duty reading newspapers and books. They were reading any kind of newspaper or books. Old yellow fragments of newspapers were precious possessions. You would find that they had even memorised the advertisements and the contents of the women's pages. Pieces of printed matter were so precious that they were read and re-read until each man could tell you the whole thing without looking at the paper. Men write letters with tiny pencil stubs that are guarded zealously and only loaned to closest friends.

I remember one day when some of the men were playing Brag. In this game each man is given three cards, and the best hand a man can hold is three aces. Six men were playing in this game. After a few unimportant deals two men got right down to earnest betting. They staked all their money. And they staked their next most precious possession—cigarettes. Then one man pitted one captured German officer's cap against two German privates' helmets. This was followed by the bet of the piece of a shell that had been taken from the wound of one of the players some months back against an iron cross which the other player had ripped off a German's breast in a night raid. In the end they had heaped up all their souvenirs, but when they attempted to wager their next quarter's pay I interrupted the game. It was no wonder they had been betting so hard. The winner held the highest possible hand of the game—three aces. But the loser had three kings.

"House" is without doubt Tommy's favourite game. It is really old-fashioned Lotto. It can be played with crowds, which is what makes it the more interesting and popular. The game consists of numbered cards with a banker who holds a bag containing the numbers which run from one to ninety. As each number is called out the men, with heads down and eyes on their cards, cover their respective numbers as they are announced, using matches, bits of paper or stones as their covering pieces. The man who has his card filled first receives the whole of the "Kitty" less a small sum which the banker appropriates as his reward for supplying the cards and calling the numbers.

"Bankers" start the games by barking in front of their trenches, and there is always lively competition. The shout with all of

them is the same, " Roll up ! Roll up !
Come along with your dough and souvenirs !
Come up with your riches and princely
treasures. Come up ! Come up ! " and occasionally a very honest one will add : " And
go away skint " (broke). Announcing the
numbers that he draws from the bag, the
banker has a language of his own. As, for
instance, the number 1 is called " bottom of
the house," number 90 " top of the house,"
and when you hear the banker shout " clickety
click," put your covering piece on 66.

It's just a little sidelight I have given you
here of the optimism and cheerfulness of the
British soldier, and my reason for presenting
this phase of his type is to claim for him that
men of such spirit can never be driven to the
despondency which accepts defeat.

CHAPTER XVII

THE RAT IN THE NIGHT

BUTTE DE WALENCOURT! Butte de Walencourt on the way to Bapaume! What a great
and thrilling story history will have to tell of
the Butte de Walencourt—merely a hill of
one hundred and fifty feet altitude and round
as the crown of a Derby hat! The days and
days when the blood of fighting men streamed
down both sides of that fiercely contested
ridge. The Germans never fought more
furiously than they did to hold the Butte de
Walencourt. They protected its flanks and
held on to it against magnificent assaults. But
more determined was the work of the South
Africans and the Durhams in the battle for
the round top of the Butte. Countless times
they made the summit, countless times they
were driven down again. Great squads of
them were slaughtered, but they would come
back the more sturdily, yes, even fanatically.
It was a specific, concrete test of the en-

durance and courage of the Boche against the British, and the British handsomely won.

It was such an awful struggle, such a thrilling victory, that in quick recognition the French Government has placed around the historic Butte de Walencourt a high wired enclosure wherein, later, is to be built a superb war memorial. Atop the round mound British commanders have already reverently erected a stone inscribed to the heroism of the South Africans and Durhams.

I had not the privilege of being in this great fight, but the Oxford and Bucks were brought up to the first line after the capture of the Butte de Walencourt, and they certainly picked out a lively job for us. It was the taking of a huge quarry behind the ridge. A dozen times in half as many days thousands of us poured into this quarry and routed the Germans, only to be literally blown out of it again by the big German guns.

In the end our army was to sweep forward, reclaiming many miles of wounded France, but there did not seem to be any prospect of advance in those days when we were tossed in and out of that quarry, each time paying heavily with lives. On the fifth

THE RAT IN THE NIGHT

day—it was in November, 1916—our battalion, badly battered, was relieved of this dangerous shuttle-cock existence and sent back to "Restville"—this particular "Restville" being pretty Beauval on the Albert-Amiens road, some thirty-one kilometres from Bapaume.

Most gratefully we "packed up our troubles in our old kit bags" and took our way down the friendly road. One of the joys of war is meeting the procession on the way to "Restville." It was all in a huge cloud of dust—marching men, thundering motor trucks and lorries, the smoothly gliding motor-cars of the officers of high command and the aviators, lumbering Paris 'buses. Shouts, yells and laughter, songs, French and English, and with the marching Tommies held not at all in check for their countless antics by the officers. For the officers, every one, had mighty good reason to be proud of their Tommies. Officers were constantly giving permission with a smiling nod to their soldiers to take advantage of invitations from the motor vehicles to the men on foot to "Get aboard, you bloomin' hiker!" And the officers themselves were being picked up by comrades. One of the happiest features was the frequent reunions of intimate friends—friends who had been wondering about the fates of one another.

The gloom of war could not annihilate the wonderful *esprit* of the good French folk of Beauval. We were back on a holiday, we were enjoying a brief respite from grim gaming with death, and they tried to hide all signs of tragedy from us. With cabaret performances in the restaurants; baths, the cool shaves, the luxury of getting manicured, concerts, vaudeville shows, public and private dining, dancing, pretty girls, general cordiality—why, God bless Beauval! As, indeed, I can remember none other of these "Restvilles" of France without finding my heart prompting the same utterance.

This period of sunshine vanished quickly enough, and November 14 found our battalion back on the front line at the Butte.

I am afraid there is nothing clairvoyant about me. I had no premonition whatsoever on leaving pleasant Beauval of the momentous episode so very nearly ahead in my life. I was all recollection then of the fine time I had had. I wanted to linger mentally with it as long as I could. Probably most delicious memory of all to the trench-worn, trench-soiled man I had been was that of the hot baths I enjoyed in Beauval. And the cold showers! I went in for about four of them the first day in, and held that average pretty nearly every other day of our rest.

Well, that and all the other pleasant things were over, and back we were to the dirty old trenches, back we were with our old comrades, the rats and moles, and Old Man Death blinking at us from the other side of No Man's Land.

We got back in the trenches on the afternoon of November 15, and we hadn't been there but two hours when I received an order to report at Colonel Reynolds's headquarters. It was a neat little dug-out he had, as spick and span as the man. The boards walling it were of spotless cleanliness, the desk at which he sat a model of orderliness, the Colonel himself calm and pleasant-voiced.

I do not mind admitting that when I left his quarters I was a very solemn-faced young man. All pretty memories of Beauval had been wiped out.

THE BIG FIGHT

I had a large responsibility and a big peril to meet.

I reflected that I had come safely through narrow and dangerous ways; my life had been spared so many times in surroundings where it seemed I had no right to hope to survive.

The assignment from my Colonel was, in brief, that we had lost touch with the 48th Toronto Regiment fighting on our left, that for the time all communications between us had mysteriously stopped. He was unaware whether the 48th had been engaged by the Germans or not. Indeed, he rather feared they had—feared they might have been struck at by a greatly superior force and possibly annihilated. The enemy had cut off telephone communications and, what was worse, had temporarily assumed an aerial superiority that had cleared our planes out of the sky.

The character and size of the German forces directly before us, the strength of their entrenchment, machine-guns and field batteries comprised, therefore, a vital matter of which he was in almost complete ignorance. As to the numerical force of the enemy, we had no thought of waiting to find this out

THE RAT IN THE NIGHT

until we were attacked. It had been the British who conducted the offensive and meant just then to continue to do so. But, as an American says, we surely ought to know " what we were up against."

He had given me the task of finding out.

Of course, you realise what that meant. I must sneak across No Man's Land in the night, I must somehow burrow my way into the enemy's territory, I must remain there long enough to get fairly accurate notes and sketches of the German position and an estimate of his number and artillery.

You will understand that it did not mean that I must cover the entire territory, and lest I might bore my reader with the military technicalities of performing such a task I will simply add that to the old soldier certain aspects are capable of equally certain deductions as to gun positions and the rest of it.

It was decided that I would start out at nine o'clock that night, and though the Germans were mercilessly strafing us, as though they were in contemplation of an onslaught of their battalions upon us, only our long-distance guns were taking up the challenge. That was a little courtesy to me. It was

enough that I would have to cross No Man's
Land under enemy fire without placing on
me the risk of losing my life by the fire of
our own guns. Small arms would have no
difficulty in carrying over the strip. No
Man's Land here was no more than five
hundred yards across. So shells, machine-
gun drums and snipers' bullets from the
Germans were ignored, our trenches making
no answer.

There had been many rains, and hardly
had I gone over the top when I realised what
lush-travelling was ahead. I soon found myself in mud up to my knees. A tiny company
of three men—a lance-corporal and two
privates—followed me out into the corpse-
strewn territory.

It looked from the very beginning as if
the Germans had suspected what was afoot.
They began making an especial display with
their star-shells the very moment after we
had started. When these flares went up, we
stood stock still and held the position steadily.
It is when you move that the light of the
star-shells limns your figure and makes you
your enemy's mark.

After the first outburst of star-shells, I

ordered my men to go on their knees and advance on all fours, thus lowering our visibility. As I sank to my knees and put out my hands one of them touched a man's face. I drew the hand back with that instinctive recoil that is uncontrollable at the touch of cold, dead flesh. I groped for the poor fellow's identification disc and papers, handed them over to the lance-corporal, and then crawled onward.

But soon the sensation of pawing over the cold faces of the dead became common to all of us. There was no shock in it any more. But we were careful to gather up their discs and papers before moving along. The new shock came when I rested my hand on the back of a man lying with his face towards the German trenches.

He moved, and I grasped him by the neck and was ready to use my trench-knife when he grunted :

" Who the hell's that?"

" Who the hell are you?" I demanded.

" Warwickshire—out on reconnaissance. Lost my way. Nearly walked into the Germans. Been wandering out two hours. Where am I, sir?"

THE BIG FIGHT

I whispered directions as to his way back.

It took us all of four hours, owing to the caution we had every instant to use, to cross that swamp of heavy mud mingled with the bodies of the fallen.

We were soon so near the enemy lines that it would have been dangerous to keep my men with me any longer. I was reluctant enough to leave them, but finally ordered them into a big shell-hole shelter where they would be well hidden from the flaring sky lights. I continued along toward the German barbed wire which the intermittent flashes plainly revealed.

I made this advance wriggling on my stomach. The men accompanying me had evidently no expectation of seeing me come back. I wasn't carrying a canteen full of confidence in that respect myself. You can't help feeling grateful in just such a moment to have had your lance-corporal and two men whisper most earnestly and sincerely, "Good luck to you, sir; good luck."

I fervently wished for that.

Mystery, weirdness and soul-sickening loneliness for me were in the picture ahead, a picture you must keep in recollection, that I could only see when it was under the uncanny illumination of the star-shells. Nature was on my side. The sky was a vast, lowering, starless mist. The meshes of barbed wire wickedly expressed their purpose as man-traps, and beyond I could see the wavering man-deep furrows in the tumbled earth. And I give you my word, not a sound. That is, not a sound to indicate the presence of hundreds of human creatures just beyond me. No sound of their moving or their breathing. There was, however, one sound, and a dreadful thing it is to hear. It was the soft scuffle of the rats among the dead.

But a few minutes later I had reason to be thankful to those rats. At the cost of a scared face and torn hands I was slowly, cautiously snapping with my wire-cutter a quiet entrance to the Boche trenches. I had gone far when I put my clippers on a certain string of wire, and my hand stiffened, my arm trembled, tickled and went numb. Simultaneously came the sharp, high ringing of a gong. They have "burglar alarms" attached to the barbed wire construction in front of the German trenches.

My salvation was in the fact that they

suspected an attack, not merely the presence of a scout. For the front line trenches began spilling everything in the way of deadliness that they had—rifle volleys, machine-gun patter, exploding bombs, and even shells. Also the Boches filled the sky with star-shells.

But when these showed no attacking force ahead the fire ceased. Still they kept up with the star-shells. I did not attempt to move. I believe that my flesh was as cold as that of any dead man as I lay there in a heavy mesh of barbed wire. I cannot imagine but that I must have been plainly in sight to some of the peering eyes from the German trench. Yet they did not see me. I did not dare look up myself to see what activity of observation took place among them.

But suddenly the firing ceased and the star-shells waned. And here's where my thankfulness to the rats comes in. I can only think that the commander of the trench de-cided that some burly rat had come into contact with the alarm wire. I know they some-times rang false alarms like that in our trenches, which are similarly equipped with bells.

When I finally dared move and stare up

through the murk, I saw two sentries posted at the entering trench. Heads and shoulders only showed. They stood statuesquely, save now and then the head of one of them bobbed in the sudden relaxation of the neck of a sleepy man.

Evidently after the big flare-up and the quieting of the alarm, these sentries didn't think themselves called upon to be particularly alert. But I was altogether too close to them to take any rash chances. I lay in the ooze fully half an hour before I dared move again. In that time the sentries disappeared.

This was good fortune, indeed. Moreover, I had come to the inner edge of the wire entanglements, and these were only loosely constructed, and I could wriggle my way through if I worked patiently. Besides, as I had full reason to believe, these inner wires were not electrically charged and would not sound an alarm.

Some hundred or more feet from the spot where I had seen the two sentries I could make out the spur of a trench, a neatly placed corner from which a machine gun could rake an attacking force. Toward the very end of that spur I went, still on my stomach. At such a time as this the likelihood of the spur being empty of the machine-gun crew was good.

I listened a long time and then risked it. I dropped into the trench. The mud in it made my fall soundless. Through this spur I picked my way to the communication trench. These communicators are always purposely blocked off in a zig-zag manner. They run on the flank of the trenches that front the enemy—run from the front to the rear trenches. To traverse one of these communication trenches is, naturally, to be able to know a great deal of the enemy's entire position. Moreover, save for sentries, and a possible but improbable patrol, the communicator is not occupied. It is the sunken roadway of the trenches.

Once inside the trenches, I was less in fear of my life than when outside. Upon the outside obviously the greatest watchfulness is exercised. The idea of an enemy within them is scarcely, if ever, entertained. I actually wormed my way past the two sentries I had seen from the outside, but who had disappeared. They had stepped down from their parapets and their heads rested drowsily against the wall of the trench. Edging past them, I held my breath and, you may be sure, was as nervous as a witch. They never even moved. But once past them I moved fast.

The utter blackness of the night was with me—was my friend. I no longer sneaked along. If observed, that would most certainly bring suspicion upon me. In the murk of the trench they would only regard me as one of their own if I passed in a natural manner as one about his quite ordinary business. Of course, I was watchful and sought not to be seen at all. The zig-zag course of the communication trenches helped this purpose along at this time.

I spent two hours in their trenches, unknown to the Germans. I made a few notes and sketches, but in the main carried the idea of the position and its strength in my mind. Once I got out and into No Man's Land again, however, I would elaborate on the sketches. In case I was killed making my way back and my comrades found my body, the papers would prove valuable, my work would be, in any event, partly done.

And there I was all unsuspected in the

quiet, gloomy trenches, where, for some reason or other, the forces again took alarm. There came the roaring medley of guns, and for me much worse—again the skies were splashed with illumination. I had just rounded a turn of the zig-zag communicator and came out in full sight of a German patrol. Two Huns faced me.

CHAPTER XVIII

THE WORST ORDEAL

I AM convinced that these two Germans I came upon were as greatly surprised as I was. I do not think I had been observed and they sent out after me. In that event, indeed, they would not have travelled together nor directly along the trench path, but would have stalked me and tried to meet me, one on either side. This is a natural plan in such hunts, for when the pursued turns to meet the attack of one man, the other has him at his mercy. But these Huns were together. And we faced one another not ten feet apart.

It certainly looked bad for me. They were both huge, robust fellows, and just about then in the glare of the night lights appeared like devils—their pale eyes gleaming through trench grime, their clothing all wrinkled and bunched about their big bodies, their mouths gone open in astonishment and showing tobacco-blackened teeth. Not that I could have looked a beauty myself, though I have to be thankful in view of what happened later that I had that morning given myself a clean shave. This fact was to save me in all probability from dreadful infection later.

Well, there must have been fully two seconds' pause, I think, in which we stood and faced each other. As I look back on it, it was a most foolish pause on my part, and the same is to be said for the pause on theirs.

With a gulp in my throat I noticed that both carried bombs—and in the very same instant I wondered why the devil I was standing there with a bomb in my own hand and not throwing it.

I let go at them—seeking to dash the bomb directly at their feet that there should be no failure of its instant explosion.

I honestly can't tell you if that bomb of mine went off. For in the very lift of my arm both Germans swung their arms into the air and hurled their bombs at me. One bomb went over my head. I am quite sure that my bomb was faulty and did not explode. The other fell directly at my feet.

I had been too long trained in that game not to know what I had to do and what I had to do in a hurry. I pounced on that bomb, and without loss of movement—without trying to stand erect and aim it, I shunted the bomb back at them with an upward toss of both hands.

And then the big thing happened—a big thing to me, but infinitely bigger to them. For that toss of the bomb cost them both their lives. I don't like to recall what I afterward saw—when smashed, bleeding and reeling, I looked to see what had become of my two enemies. The truth is they were blown to pieces. One man's severed head was nearly at my feet. The star-shell showed it to me. It was staring up at me with a frightful grimace. Their bodies were scattered in that pathway as though they had been hacked to pieces by an axe—worse than that—as though they had been hacked to pieces by an axe with a roughened, dull edge.

In the first of the explosion, of course, I knew nothing of this. I was receiving my own crippling from the back-blast of the German bomb I had hurled at them. There was a glare and a sudden shock in my face as though I had been struck on the mouth with a sledge-hammer. Of course, I went down. But as far as my own recollection goes I was not knocked unconscious, and I was immediately afterward sitting up in the pathway while I coughed and sputtered blood from a mouth in which all the upper teeth had been cracked or blown out and the upper jaw itself broken. Then, as the earth* stopped swaying, I knew my right arm was numb and stared at it. My hand was a red mangle. At the same time there came a realisation of hellish paroxysms of pain on the left side of my face and biting savagely at my left arm. I touched my face with my left hand and instinctively drew the fingers away in horror. The flesh of my face was raw.

My long soldier's training was my salvation now. I doubt whether without it I should have known just what to do and have done it with the promptness and precision of a man used to obeying military orders. At any rate, once I realised my condition, once I had looked upon my red, smashed hand, the slit sleeve, and the flesh all torn beneath it, I immediately reached with my serviceable hand into the little pocket in the inside of my jacket for the precious phial of iodine.

THE WORST ORDEAL

Subconsciously I lifted the bottle with the idea of pulling the cork out with my teeth—good, strong, wholesome teeth they had been—when I realised the maimed condition of my mouth. Then you may believe I hesitated. But I did not dare risk the loss of any of that fluid. I must get antiseptic on my wounds. Here I was on the wrong side of No Man's Land and in full knowledge of how much mercy I might expect from the Germans if I issued a call for help that would disclose a scout in their territory, and beside that scout the dismembered bodies of their own dead. Again, if I lost the contents of this magic phial I must face the ordeal of dying in agonies of raging, infected wounds—die like a wounded rat in the enemy's country. It would not do to risk breaking the bottle against a stone in the hope of transferring most of its contents to my wounds. There was only too little of the fluid as it was.

So, red and torn as my mouth was, the upper jaw broken, I put the cork to my lips, determined to stand whatever shock of pain the effort must cost me. I did not know it then, but curiously enough when this wound came to be examined it was found that although the shock of the back-blast had broken my upper jaw and cracked or blown away all the teeth in it, my lower jaw and teeth were intact. There wasn't a tooth injured. I don't remember exactly, but the escape of my under-jaw in the explosion indicates that I had probably opened my mouth to utter some yell or taunt at my enemies as we fought.

Well, somehow, I got that cork between what was left of my teeth, closed on it, and drew it. Hurt? I was blind with pain in the process. My one good hand shook, and I all but dropped the bottle. But then, I was in such a whirl of pain anyway that the shock of more could not possibly destroy me.

I could not lift the right arm or move the hand, of which I now observed that the entire thumb and base of it down to the wrist had been blown off. But while holding the bottle of iodine in my good hand, I managed to bare the entire wound from the torn sleeve and shirt sleeve that clung to it. I poured the biting iodine carefully all over the wound. It stung poignantly, but there had come over me a certain desperation that seemed to give me unlimited power to resist pain, made me in an astonishing degree impervious to it.

The arm was bleeding in gouts, and I knew this had to be stopped, and stopped quickly, or it would not take many minutes to make a dead man of me. Already I was beginning to experience a daze of weakness. So I had to go through another agonising ordeal.

I got out my handkerchief, and, again employing my wounded mouth to aid my serviceable hand, tied the handkerchief around my arm in the manner of a tourniquet—a performance in which I had expert training and practice—made a final loop, found a knife in my pocket, inserted it into the loop, and, though my arm throbbed excruciatingly in appeal for gentleness, turned the lever relentlessly until I knew the flow of blood must be greatly checked if not entirely stopped.

Now you must not think this took me any great time. I did it shakily but in greatest haste. For common sense gave its warning that the explosion of the bomb in territory near their batteries must soon bring investigators. And what I knew they did to soldiers they caught in their man-traps I knew they would as certainly do to me if I was found—just cold-bloodedly and in Hun fashion slay and mutilate me. I heard the grumblings and sharp mutterings of men coming up from a dug-out. And when I say in Hun fashion I mean something horrible —more horrible than even the world has yet learned.

And in this moment, crucial moment of my life, I leaped out of the trench, and in the same instant I saw my saviour. I hope it is all right to call a mud-hole a saviour. There it was behind a clump of ragged bushes. I like to reflect now that it was one of the shells from our own guns, as they sought out this battery of the enemy, that had made for me this refuge.

I stumbled and plodded for this mud-hole. Most gratefully I sank into it. I threw myself into it fully, a dead weight, that I might sink the deeper into it. I didn't in the least mind the pain to my wounds that the fall cost me. I then began, with all the speed I could muster, slapping the mud all over me as in happier days at the ocean side I had buried myself in the hot, dry sands.

I revelled in this reeking, black muck. And with good reason. As I sank deeper and deeper into it and slapped it over my body, then over my face, when I was submerged in the black, glutinous, offensive pudding so that only my nose stuck out, a nose smeared also to conform to the surface colour of the muck-hole—well, then and only then I began to feel that I had a chance for my life.

A mud-hole may be an ignoble thing, but God's blessing on this one. It proved, as I have said, my life-saver. I had hardly thoroughly concealed myself in the black mess when a dozen soldiers came treading the path and the surrounding land—came wearily, some with rifles, some with bombs.

I had dared to leave an eye open at the surface of my hiding-place and saw them coming. But I did not continue this foolishness. Well enough I realised that just this eye—its gleam and movement (even in the night) might attract notice, especially of men keenly watchful. I closed that eye—and with the merest movement sank my head deeper into the mud. I had hoped to keep my nostrils sufficiently clear of mud to breathe, but in this action they also clogged up, and I must have strangled if my enemies had delayed long in the vicinity of my mud-hole.

But they saw the dismembered bodies of their comrades, and could see no enemy wounded nearby. They concluded that, escaping our guns, no enemy would remain long in the territory, and were equally certain he would not continue his advance toward their batteries. It was natural for them to judge he had retreated for his own lines. This, I suppose, is the way their minds worked and that they continued the pursuit to No Man's Land until it became dangerous to follow it farther, and abandoned the hunt.

I don't know. For I did not see them when they departed. I took no chances on peering out. I took only one chance, and that was to thrust my nose into the air to keep myself from strangling, but I did this most cautiously.

I was left secure for the time at least in my mud-hole.

And I was to exist in this wallow for three

days. I afterward found out that it was three days. How long I had no idea at the time. There were hours of torture, hours, I presume, of coma, hours of delirium, in which I thought I underwent crazy experiences, had amazing visions, dreamed both horrible and beautiful dreams. I could not at any time have been bereft of all my senses, for I clearly retain a memory of these mental fantasies, none but two very clearly, but the others, while vague, are still not altogether indefinable.

Some time passed and no bayonet came thrusting into my body, and no bomb that would rend me and my muddy blankets into a ghastly mess had fallen. The pain suddenly quieted, and a tremendous languor seized me.

Immediately I was possessed of a deadly fear of falling asleep. I feared in the first place the peril and horror of the man-eating rat. I feared as well that I would sink so deeply into the mud-hole that I would suffocate as I slept. Yet I realised that it could not be of so very great depth or I must have long ago gone beneath the surface as in a quicksand. I remembered the general aspect of the gap as torn by the shell. It had been a small shell. The gap was not large. And was probably shallow. Besides, the ground beneath me below the mud had a reassuring firmness.

But had the mud in the hole been of a depth for me to drown in, it would have made no difference then. A weariness too intense to permit consideration of life and death gripped me. For all I knew, it was death itself. What I did know was that I could not fight it. I simply passed out.

For my eventual survival from the predicament I now found myself in I can only give credit to the good physical condition I was in when my injuries befell me, the injuries that were to put me out of the big game for good, send me to " Blighty," and to get me honours from King and country reverently to be prized, and which in my greatest imaginings I had not dreamed of winning. A practical, regular soldier doesn't frequently dream of such things. It is your amateur soldier who is most filled with such aspirations. Not that he hasn't a right to entertain them, coddle them, and try to act on them, for they have led many new-made soldiers into great and brave accomplishments. I don't mean such dreams and aspirations are bad for a man. They are distinctly good. I only mean that with regulars like myself soldiering is his cold, hard business, and he isn't given to enhancing it with romantic imaginings.

But now I was to take a turn at imaginings myself—the wildest! I suppose I fought again at least a hundred times my duel with the two Germans, who grew to a giant size in some of my dreams, and always their countenances were a thing of horror—pale eyes shining through grime, stubbled chins and lips, cracked lips apart, with blackened, fang-like teeth showing. Sometimes they beat me. They would have me down and be kneeling on my chest. And one of them would have a knife out with which to slash my throat. And I'd come out of such a horror writhing and screaming.

Then, again, I would suffer the keenest tortures because of the roaring of guns— imaginary guns at that, I suppose they were, smashed at my ears and racked my burning head. I would find myself screaming at them to desist.

THE BIG FIGHT

Then I had fine, serene dreams when I travelled through a great land—I can't tell what land, merely Dreamland—that was all at peace.

There were no ugly shell marks in it. There were no frightened, helpless women, no whimpering children. There were bright sunlight, huge herds of peaceful cattle, and I passed (I don't know how—in auto, horseback, aeroplane, or on wings) beautiful, happy old farm-houses, saw playing children, and the only time I had war in my mind was when I came upon a group of old men at the fire of a famous ancient inn I knew in Ireland. And what they were having to say about the big fight was to marvel that such a great tragedy could ever have occurred. And I stood beside them and wept at my memories of the ghastly war.

But the master dream—one that seemingly never left me, I have to confess, was of a girl. Of course, a wonderful girl. It seems that this dream was always hovering in my brain, that it was always recurring to displace the other dreams. This girl was of changeless aspect. She was blue-eyed, always blue-eyed. These eyes were always blessing

me with the assurance that everything in the
end was to come out right. Her mouth was
a marvel of kindliness and tenderness. I
suppose my fevered brain was simply evolv-
ing the ideal girl that had always been in my
mind. At any rate, this girl was my angel
then—the angel of the mud-hole, if you will,
but she certainly was God-sent to me while
my mind wandered and my body, without my
will or direction, was putting up its fight for
life.

Even in such times as I came into possession of my senses she was still only half-veiled
from me. I could close my eyes and bring
her vision back at will.

I had my lucid moments right enough—
startlingly clear mental periods when I
realised the desperation of my plight, when
I despaired of ever getting out of the wretched
black wallow alive, and when I had thought
of food.

Here I was not wholly bereft. Of course,
going on such an expedition as had brought
me into my present situation, I had fore-
thought to carry emergency rations. I had
in my pockets four biscuits and seven cakes
of chocolate.

THE BIG FIGHT

My clothes were soon soaked through and through with the ooze of mud. The biscuits in one pocket were as mush, the chocolate cakes also, and the biscuits had, because of the muddy water, turned the same colour as the chocolate cakes.

I was thankful for the softened condition of both. My wounded mouth was swollen and inflamed. I could hardly move my lips. I never could have broken between my torn gums a bite off a biscuit. But because they had been thoroughly wet I could suck at them and draw the bits of pasty food down and swallow them. And likewise with the chocolate.

In these clear-headed moments I well enough knew myself to be the victim of fever, and I was hoping and praying that if it ever left me I might find myself with strength enough to crawl out of my black bed of mud and make at least a fight to get back to my own, to protection, to the hospital, and perhaps—yes, for all my wounds, for all the terrors and horrors I had been through, I did hope I would be able eventually to get back into the big fight. And this is not heroics. It is because I am a man, and no man could have seen the crimes of the Germans I have seen and not want to fight the Boches as long as he could stand.

Fortunately, thoughts of food had only come to me in my sane moments, and I had therefore been able rigidly to adhere to my plan to eat sparingly—only a portion of a biscuit at a time, only a portion of a chocolate cake. On the morning of the third day I still had fragments of each left.

The mud-hole was the only fountain to slake my thirst, for my water-bottle had been blown away with my thumb and other fragments of my flesh by the bomb. I wasn't drinking from a crystal spring. I would press the mud down and make a small hole that filled with stale, black water that tasted even worse than it looked. But it was, for all that, delicious to my fevered, wounded mouth. Drinks of it put more life in me than ever "trench rum" did.

And I cannot help but believe that my good old mud-hole had done more for me than conceal me from my enemies. I believe it acted as a poultice for my wounds in the three days, or nearly three days, in which I soaked in it. My fevers had come on at night most violently. I honestly do not remember ever having experienced a thorough chill. I was cold and clammy in my waking hours, but never cold to the point of suffering acutely on that score.

But my food was gone, and though my head was light and my wounded arm hurting me intensely, I found myself on the night of this third day feeling that possibly I had acquired strength for the five hundred yards' journey back to our lines. In my weakened condition I had to think of how the obstacles, quite aside from danger from the Germans, would impede me in the night. I mean the shell-holes, the sections of barbed wire left upstanding in No Man's Land, and the countless dead bodies I might fall over, the ravenous rats which might attack me. But to have attempted to crawl away in the daytime would have meant certain death.

It may seem a strange statement, but it is true—I have the dead men of No Man's Land to thank for the fact that I am still living.

There was a mist over the land the night I made my escape. The mist decided me that the time had come to "carry on" unless I could resign myself to rot to death in the mud-hole.

Surely the fog would last until I could stagger out of immediate German territory and merge myself into the torn and blasted waste of No Man's Land.

I decided to make the try.

The first twenty feet I walked seemed as far as I was ever going to get. I was breathless, giddy, and my legs were almost as irresponsible to direction as was my wounded arm whenever I tried to raise it. I sat, or rather fell, into some smashed shrubbery, and rocked and wept in despair. But that spell of weakness passed and I got to my feet again.

To my surprise—you must understand my long imprisonment in the mud-hole had made my mind almost as wavery as my legs—my legs seemed stronger. Of course, they would. The confinement in the mud-hole had benumbed them. My feet began to tingle with an almost acute pain. But as I continued to move along I walked the more easily. But I was dazed and I was continuously falling over obstacles of brush or loose stones.

With death threatening behind you can perform marvels, and it is my only explana-

tion of how I ever made the journey I did.
I can't attempt to tell this journey in detail.
It was a nightmare of pain and horrors,
myself more like a sleepwalker than anything
else as I endured its hardships.

As I think back on it it seems to me that
I was always swaying, always stumbling.
But I remember finding myself well out in
No Man's Land and flat on my back where
I had blindly fallen.

Then the reek of the dead brought me
staggering to my feet and to my senses. I
looked about me like a frightened, bewildered
child. The things I saw were so horrible—
the dead, sprawled as they were struck down,
distorted, maimed in so many ways, made a
spectacle so awful that I cried out : " Good
God ! I'm not going to become one of these.
God help me ! I must not. God help me."

And I went tottering along.

And that is why I have said that if it were
not for the dead I would not now be among
the living. For whenever my strength
seemed altogether spent, whenever I began
telling myself it was no use, that I'd have to
give up, my eyes would turn upon the constant spectacle of the dead in No Man's Land,

as the bursting lights in the sky revealed them.
Some of them were headless. Some hung
grotesquely on patches of barbed-wire entanglement that had not been smashed down
by the shells of previous battle, some—but
detail of this sort is perhaps too frightful to
even simply describe. All I know is that,
every time I was ready to surrender, the sight
of these piteous dead men nerved me to go
on. I would not join them. I would not
become as they were. I would not fall and
lie there to fester and rot, to become a
noisome thing.

Positively, unreservedly, it was these men,
who had already given their lives for their
countries, whom I have to thank for the pre-
servation of my own. Their grim presence
drove me on and on.

Evidently I had escaped from my mud-
hole unobserved by the enemy. No bullets
had sung after me; there had never been a
sign of pursuit.

But now I had to consider a new danger.
Weak as I was, feeling that every next step
must be my last, I realised that it would not
do for me to go marching straight for the
Canadian trenches which I knew to be almost

straight beyond. The 48th Toronto Regiment were there. In such case I might expect them to do for me what the Germans had failed to do. I might expect a clutter of bullets to strike me down.

They could not know me from a Boche. I was caked all over with mud. I was a strange figure. And I well knew that so many had been the schemes and strategies of the Boche spies that in all probability the Canadians would shoot first and inquire regarding me afterward.

I had to rake my confused mind for a recollection of the lie of the land along the trenches, for a recollection of the secret paths by which they might be flanked and then approached. I never put in a greater effort of will. And finally I remembered.

After that it was just a long stumble. I was falling like a clown at almost every step. I would faint and awaken to find myself flat on my back or on my face.

But in the end I huddled in a narrow pathway so near a Canadian trench that I could hear some chap singing. It didn't help me any that he was singing a hymn and singing it most lugubriously.

THE WORST ORDEAL

Daylight had come.

My whole thought and effort now were in gathering sufficient strength to utter a yell loud enough to carry to that trench. I was panting. It was agony for me to move my lips. And weak! Good heavens, I would have fallen over at the kick of a rabbit!

I breathed hard, tried to fill my lungs, and after a wait of ten minutes, I am sure, let go my "yell." It was the most pitiful "yell" ever made. It was as slight as a sick infant's cry. What I had tried to shout was "Oh, Canadians!" Of course, none heard it. So I waited there, resting another fifteen minutes. I tried again to shout. To my surprise my voice came out strong and loud :

"Oh, Canadians!"

With my last strength I repeated the cry, and it came loudly again : "Oh, Canadians! Oh, Canadians!"

"Who's there?"

I tried to answer and couldn't.

Then a tall fellow with set bayonet ran down the pathway. He saw my helpless condition readily enough and strode straight for me.

THE BIG FIGHT

"British officer," I was able to whisper. "Wounded."

"Cheero, sir," he answered. "Lots of help for you here."

He lifted me, got a long, strong arm under my shoulders, and began leading me along the little path.

And just then the damned battery of the Huns, from which I had so laboriously, painfully and at times helplessly fled, opened up an intensive fire. Not this battery alone, but scores all along the line. But I thought only of that particular battery just then. And no sooner had I thought of it than a shell burst almost upon us. We were slammed to the ground. A burst of light swept the entire position. My companion's sturdy support fell from me and he uttered a scream. I stared toward him as the dust and smoke cleared away. Simultaneously with the shock of the shell explosion a sniper's explosive bullet had struck him in the left arm. The dum-dum bullet tore the arm completely from his shoulder. He was looking dazed but conscious.

"See, I'm hit!" he said in childlike astonishment.

THE WORST ORDEAL

"Sorry," I whispered at him. "Sorry that I was the cause."

He nodded and tried to smile.

"It's all in the game," he answered, and fell over.

There came a rush of men out of the trench to our rescue, and they carried us both into its protection. They pushed a cigarette between my lips, the first thing that's always done for a wounded comrade in the trenches, but I was too weak and sick to want that small, immediate comfort. The cigarette hung from my wounded lips. I tried to thank them, but could say nothing. I was making a desperate fight to hold on to consciousness.

CHAPTER XIX

BLIGHTY

My body was battered, half-frozen, gone altogether helpless, but I am grateful that my mind remained faithful to its task. In fact, it seemed to scorn the state of my body and was extraordinarily clear and acute. Every fact, impression, knowledge of any sort that I had obtained on my venture into the German position arrayed itself neatly and precisely in my thoughts. The Canadians wanted to rush me off immediately on a stretcher, but after the refreshment of a drink of water I felt quite able to complete my work by reporting to the proper officers the information I had gained. Two were soon at my side, racing through a communication trench from their dug-out.

I indicated to them an inside pocket of my tunic where were the maps I had made roughly in the darkness, but which I knew would be significant to them. My broken and shattered jaw made talking something of an agony, but I was able to bear it and mumble what additional knowledge I had to yield.

These fellow-officers were extravagant in praise of my adventure and almost embarrassed me by their solicitude, insisting on lifting me with their own hands into the stretcher that had been brought, and on walking beside it to the entrance to the hospital, which was on the third trench line. It was no easy task for the stretcher bearers. To reach this hospital they had to descend long, rude, tortuous stairways. The hospital room was one hundred feet underground. Its only illumination was by candlelight, and you got the impression of mystery and tragedy. In the dim glow the white-robed doctors and grey-robed nurses moved noiselessly on a tan bark-covered floor. Their noiselessness made all the more distinct sharp moans from my fellow-wounded. There were not cots enough for all. Some had been laid on pallets of straw.

Three men were terribly wounded. One had both legs off. The chest and shoulders of another had been torn raw and half his chin smashed away. My restless eyes saw the face of another the orderlies were just bandaging. His eyes had been ripped out.

Some months before I had heard an anecdote of a poilu who had lost both hands. And when a sympathetic Frenchwoman would have commiserated him for this dire misfortune he unconsciously by old habit, and therefore none the less pitifully, raised the stumps to make a true Gallic gesture with both hands that were not there, and he said to her :

" Madame, it is right that you should pity me. My friend Anatole gave his life. I was but privileged to give my hands for France."

I'm Irish and I'm emotional, and that splendid reply stuck hard and fast in my admiration. It is but natural that a man should feel certain moments of keen bitterness when he realises he has been crippled for life. But if I had had the slightest impulse to self-pity, which I had not, the reply of that poilu would have shamed it out of me.

And if not that, there was the sight of the three men in this dim, subterranean hospital so much more terribly wounded than I. I could only think of myself as having been fortunate. A doctor had looked at my wounded arm, murmured something to the orderly, shaken his head discouragingly. But I remembered that I had not only escaped thus far with my life but had the further good fortune of having a clean, healthy body to fight for me—for my life, and, possibly— I didn't go farther than to think it out that way—possibly I might not have to lose my arm.

To add to my optimism I soon began to know the first experiences of a transposition from hell to heaven. From the hell of the dirt and grime, disease, vermin, and death of the trenches to the heaven of the sweet peace and tenderness that sick men feel under the gentle ministrations of noble women.

They were wonderfully expert in cutting away and stripping my mud-soaked and rotted uniform and other clothing from my body. I hardly felt a pang when they lifted and snipped away the cloth from the sleeve of my burned left arm and cleansed the wound of my long-tortured and smashed right hand and forearm. I could almost smile when, having washed my torn mouth, they further cleansed it with antiseptics that stung cruelly.

THE BIG FIGHT

With these same rapid, clever hands they rubbed my body from head to feet with anti-frost grease, and I grinned as after that they rolled me up in cotton-wool, just as if I were some big, foolish sort of a doll to be boxed and sold at Christmas. I continued to grin, for after that they made a Teddy Bear of me, pulling over the cotton-wool thick, full length woollen tights and a big, stuffy woollen jersey.

One of the nurses was a young woman with blue eyes—just the sort of blue eyes I had thought of when I was lying in fever out in the mud-hole; the other a middle-aged woman of serene deportment. The young nurse, catching me grinning, smiled back at me, but the older nurse looked puzzled.

"What in the world," she said in her cool, even voice, "can that young rascal find to laugh at in such a time as this?"

"Isn't it splendid," said the young nurse, "that he can laugh?" And she nodded toward me with a knowing smile, and—bless my soul! what crazy irresponsibilities our emotions are!—I suddenly found my eyes filled with tears.

She came back to me a few seconds later with a glass of hot milk which I had perforce to drink through a tube, and, thank the Lord, she took no notice of my wet eyes.

I had been two hours in the underground cave hospital when I was transferred to a stretcher and sent off, borne by four giant Scots with two other Scots accompanying to act as reliefs in the task of carrying me half a mile or more to another station. They could not have been more kindly and attentive to gentleness in carrying me had they been the bearers of a princeling. It was rough walking, most of it more than ankle deep in mud, and when one of the bearers stumbled, went to his knees and nearly shot me off the stretcher, one of the relief men strode forward in great anger :

" Make way oot o' that, Jock," he commanded, " and gie me the handle. D'ye no think the puir officer already hurt enough?"

I would say for him after he took hold that never once did he stumble.

They finally landed me safely, and with fewer jars and jolts than were to have been expected, at a small station where I became a passenger on a curious ambulance. It was made of a stretcher swung between two enormous wheels that one sees on rustic carts. An old fat horse drew this ambulance. The stretcher swung gently between the wheels as he stolidly plodded over rough ground, sometimes muddy, sometimes rocky. It was slow moving, for night had come, and all along our course shell-craters, which would capsize the ambulance did it slump into them, had to be guarded against.

My wounds sometimes set viciously to work to give me pain, but again would show mercy. I found a certain soothing effect in the swing of the hammock. And I stared up at the stars that were brilliant, and thought how wonderful it was that I was alive at all, and reflected whether, if I were to be able to fight no more, my country might not make use of me in drilling her other young sons to "carry on" in her tremendous and noble cause.

The good old fat horse bore me two miles on my way and brought me to a motor ambulance. It had three bunks in it, and two were already occupied. When I was placed in this ambulance I began to think that perhaps I had been premature in believing my life saved. For I knew enough of ambulances to know that the bottom bunk is reserved for the carrying of the most dangerously wounded, and it was into the bottom bunk they slid me.

I am perfectly willing that Henry Ford should have such advertising as may be from me, for it was an ambulance of his make I rode in, and the fact that it could proceed at all over the roads we had to travel, and often enough no roads whatsoever—in and out of gullies, shell-holes, over sunken fields, up pathless hills, and finally land me at No. 9 Clearing Station of the Red Cross, certainly earns it honest commendation.

The ambulance drivers told me that the foul-fighting Huns had attacked this big frame hospital only a few days before, and although their shells had not struck, the shocks from the explosions had snapped the slender threads by which three dangerously wounded men were clinging to life.

I was no sooner in the hospital than I was to discover that the Canadians had sent ahead such glowing accounts of my exploit that in this hospital I found myself regarded as a hero and made much of, though you wouldn't think a "hero" would create much of a sensation in this particular place whose every cot had again and again been occupied by heroes.

One of the first at my bedside was the Rev. Michael Adler, chaplain of the Jews, and through his friendly offices I was enabled to send cards to my friends in England and Australia and other countries, telling them I was dangerously wounded, but most strongly hoped to pull through. Particular communications were sent to my old commander, Col. A. Gilbey, and to Maj. Lionel Rothschild in London.

Again I passed into the hands of deft nurses. They removed my innumerable wrappings, cleansed me anew and—another transposition from hell to heaven—laid me in a spotless white linen-draped bed! I was weak as a wounded rabbit by this time, perhaps, but nevertheless I was able to get a thrill out of this! A bed all white, clean, sweet and neat!

If only a wounded soldier out of the dirty trenches could turn poet! He could knock the spots off a lot of things other poets have written about love and springtime and a' that and a' that! He could make the song of a thrush sound like a beaten tin pan by his ode to a little white cot and the angels that hover round it!

Then three earnest, quick-eyed doctors looked at my smashed arm. Two of them were young men, the third middle-aged. It was he who finally left the group that stepped off from my bedside for consultation, and said:

"My boy, I'm afraid it will have to come off—the hand, perhaps part of the arm."

I had expected the verdict, yet I would be dishonest not to admit that I was shocked and horrified just the same.

My thumbless right hand had been laid bare of its bandages. I looked at it, maimed as it was, and shook my head.

"I don't want to lose my hand, doctor," I said, "what is left of my hand. Certainly not my arm."

"Then," he said, briefly enough, but with greatest kindness, "I cannot be sure that I can save your life."

So I told him that I had always been careful of my body, had lived cleanly against every temptation, and asked him if that could not be considered to count for me.

"Yes," he said. "What you tell me certainly makes a difference. Yet I am hardly willing to advise you to take the chance."

A sudden confidence obsessed me.

"I am willing to take the chance," I told him. "I know I can fight it through."

He looked at me in a fatherly, studious fashion for several seconds.

"Fallon," he said, in a very ordinary tone of voice, "I think you will."

It wasn't more than an hour after that when I was on the operating table, for the infected fragments of my thumb had to be cut away, and if the arm was to be saved at all other surgical work was necessary. As to the success of these operations it is only necessary to say that I still have my arm and my hand, though it is thumbless. For a long time this right arm of mine was a useless appendage dangling from my shoulder. But week by week it became more like a living member of my body.

When I was given an anæsthetic for the major operation, I suddenly got the absurd notion of counting—counting from one to nineteen. Well, it was "twenty" before I woke up.

BLIGHTY

When I did so it was to find myself squeezing for dear life the hand of the nurse beside me. As I batted my eyes she said :

" You bad boy, you're hurting me."

" I thought I was in heaven holding the hand of an angel ! " I gasped at her, not making much of a success, however, of this attempt to be gay.

But she chuckled—the nicest, softest chuckle you ever heard.

" That," she told me, " will be sufficient of your blarney."

Then I had a long sleep. And when I awakened I was weak as an infant, and for days fed like one—hot milk out of a bottle, from a baby's tube affixed.

They told me afterward the fight for my life was a hard one—on one or two occasions desperate. I know myself there were times when I thought the fight was going to finish against me.

But something happened that would brace any man. The nurse with the lovely chuckle brought a paper to me and read it, pausing to make every word clear, distinct, impressive. I could feel new blood racing into my veins at every word.

THE BIG FIGHT

For she read to me the order of recommendation for the decoration of Lieutenant David Fallon with the Military Cross, as sent out from my Battalion Headquarters, forwarded to Field-Marshal Haig at Grand Headquarters, approved by the great British leader, and then forwarded for posting in all British commands.

And it read :

Lieut. David Fallon, Oxfordshire and Buckinghamshire Light Infantry. Though dangerously wounded, he carried out a most daring reconnaissance and gained much valuable information. He set a splendid example throughout.

I don't think science would have failed me. But if it were going to, here was the magic cure.

CHAPTER XX

THERE would be little gratitude in me if I did not set down in this story of my experiences the delightful kindnesses and unremitting attention which came to me after, on the score of a fighting man, I had become useless to my country. For the country certainly wasn't ungrateful. Famous surgeons were giving attention constantly to the thorough healing and saving of my arm; there followed constant treatments to destroy the paralysis which afflicted it, treatments which promise in time I shall have the use of it restored.

And quite as remarkable was the repair of my broken jaw, the extraordinary skill of dentistry by which the broken teeth were re-made, the jaw itself braced and placed firm by golden bands. When the work was completed I was overjoyed to find that I could articulate without the slightest impediment, and masticate as thoroughly and easily as ever I could. For a long time, however, I was restricted to mere liquid food, feeding out of a tube as if David Fallon were thirty weeks instead of thirty years old.

From the hospital where the operation on my arm had been performed I was taken, in company with scores of other injured, in a battalion of motor-cars to a train at Albert, whence we travelled to Rouen, where I remained for several weeks at No. 8 General Hospital, and where my attending physician was Captain Page, and my nurse Miss Templey, a cousin of Major Templey, all of whom I had known in India.

I was quickly recovering my strength, and was finally sent aboard the *Caledonia* for the trip to Southampton. They had spotless clean bunks for us and scores of charming young women—young college women who had left their studies to serve in the Voluntary Aid Detachment. Imagine the peace and pleasure for men who were just returning from hell to have such companionship, to listen to songs beautiful and soft where they had been listening to the scream of shells, to hear voices sweet and gentle where they had been for months hearing only the sharp moans

of the wounded or the raucous voices of
authority raised in deadly emergencies!
Talk of Nirvana at its best! This was something better!

Arrangements for our reception at Southampton were as smoothly efficient and kindly
as had been our transportation and treatment
in France. Individually, good fortune was
attending every little distance in my journey.
Taken to London, I found myself billeted in
the home of Lady Carnarvon in Bryanston
Square. She had turned her beautiful resi-
dence into a hospital, and there I was quartered in a spacious apartment with Lieutenant McDonald of a Lancashire regiment,
who had a smashed leg, and Captain Fred
Monk, M.C., who had also a smashed leg and
had lost an arm.

But he was very cheerful regarding the
situation, and so was McDonald. On the
train for the wounded and also aboard the
Caledonia you hardly heard any talk of war.
Everybody was sick of it. They wanted to
talk about anything but war. But here at
Lady Carnarvon's, in the days that followed,
naturally our memories came crowding back.
And we went over our hardships, the thrills

we had experienced, and then inevitably the panorama would sweep our vision of the sections of No Man's Land we had seen with its piled and distorted dead, and one of us, without feeling the necessity of telling the others of what he was thinking, would as inevitably say :

" Well, we are very lucky beggars after all."

These would usually be the thoughts in the twilight hour, and then in would walk our smiling, rosy-cheeked Irish tease of a nurse, Miss Anne O'Laughlin—all the nurses at Lady Carnarvon's were Irish and therefore for me the more charming—preceding an orderly with tea things. She'd sit and smile and jest, and make an hour or more dash by so pleasantly that—well, we very well knew at those times that we were very lucky beggars indeed.

Then when I was on my feet I was sent to Lady Furness's hospital at Harrogate, and there I spent a delightful convalescence, and there it was that I received the dispatch from the Lord Chamberlain of His Majesty to appear at Buckingham Palace for decoration.

Colonel Holland, D.S.O., of the Indian

Army, commandant at Lady Furness's hospital, personally brought me the dispatch, and seemed as proud of it as I was, for I had been one of his youngsters in the ranks in India.

The dispatch read :

Your attendance is required at Buckingham Palace on Wednesday the twenty-fifth inst. at ten-thirty o'clock a.m. Service dress. Regret that no one except those to be invested can be admitted to the Palace. Please telegraph acknowledgment.

THE LORD CHAMBERLAIN, London.

I went to London as the guest of some old friends named Morris, and accompanied by Miss Dora Morris, daughter of the family, and Miss Norah Dixon, of Australia, motored to Buckingham Palace, arriving at one of the entrances, and then not being certain as to which of the roadways of approach to the Palace I should take.

I had the problem solved for me by a "bobby" who, with an agonised expression, ran toward our car, frantically waving his white gloves.

"Out of the way quickly, sir!" he shouted.

I was pardonably nettled.

THE BIG FIGHT

"But I have been commanded here to receive the Military Cross."

He saluted, but shouted to the chauffeur :

"To the left—to the left. Good Lor', the King's behind you!"

Of course, the chauffeur responded with alacrity, and as His Majesty went by, flanked by an admiral and a general, I saluted, and the salute was returned by all three.

Then the "bobby," still flustered, directed my car along the right road, and a few minutes later the young ladies left me at the entrance to Buckingham Palace. No arrangements for spectators are made for these ceremonies, none invited.

I was relieved of my cap and stick by an august-looking footman, who whispered to me to retain my gloves, and I passed into a large reception-room where there were already some two hundred soldiers, officers and men of the ranks, summoned for a like purpose as myself, and within the next minute nearly one hundred more. The furnishings of the salon were Victorian, the upholstering well worn. Big paintings were on the walls, illustrating most of the picturesque events in the life of Queen Victoria.

HONOURED BY THE KING

Among those assembled were six men who had achieved the rare distinction of the Victoria Cross, more than a hundred who had earned the Distinguished Service Order, and the remainder M.C.s. The majority of us showed on our bodies the marks of the experiences we had been through. There were more than a score who had been blinded, more than half a hundred who had to use crutches. Nearly every face was scarred.

The V.C.s and D.S.O.s were directed to the right side of the room and we to the left, and then the Lord Chamberlain called :

" Order, gentlemen ! "

When we had come to attention he said :

" This is the order of procedure you will observe. Names will be called with regard to seniority and alphabetically. You will walk in file as your names are called and you will then proceed under the escort of chamberlains until you come to the door of the room where His Majesty is presenting the honours. You will keep the left hand gloved and bare the right. As you enter His Majesty's presence you will turn to the left and be facing the King. As your turn comes, I will read out from the *Gazette* the reason for which honour is to be conferred on you. Then you will advance two steps and bow. When your medal has been placed upon you by His Majesty, who will, of course, shake hands and speak to you, you will step two paces to the rear, bow, turn to the right, and leave by the right exit."

As the names were being called attendants passed among us, affixing to the left, on the breast of our tunics, golden pins on which, later, His Majesty would hang the medals.

When my turn came and I had observed the instructions and stood before the King, it was to face a small, slightly stooped gentleman of quiet, kindly-eyed, friendly demeanour and most unassuming, despite the rather gorgeous general's uniform he wore. An admiral stood at his left; a general at his right. Each had in his possession the medals to be awarded the men of his particular branch of the Imperial service.

My right arm was still perforce in a sling. The King, quickly noting it, extended his left hand to me and with my left hand I clasped it.

"You are to regain the use of your arm, I hope," he said.

THE BIG FIGHT

stick, and stepped out to the entrance, where the motor car was summoned, and I started back to the home of my friends. My young lady companions had graciously awaited me in the car.

Yet I rode back not altogether happily. I had come through with my life, I was maimed but by no means crippled for future usefulness, my nerves and mind were unimpaired, I had the King's decoration on my coat, but for all that I felt an actual keen pang of lonesomeness. I was out of it—out of the big fight.

PRINTED BY CASSELL & COMPANY, LIMITED, LA BELLE SAUVAGE, LONDON, E.C.4

F30.1218

HONOURED BY THE KING

"The doctors are not sure, your Majesty," I answered, "but I am optimistic."

"I am sure you will," he said, and, glanc-ing at the scar on my left cheek, asked me if my eyes had been affected. His voice was genuinely sympathetic; he appeared really interested.

I told him in this regard I had been most fortunate—my sight was not in any serious degree affected.

"I am happy to hear it. And how have you been treated in your illness? Are there any complaints that should be made in regard to arrangements for the wounded and their treatment?"

"I have only the greatest praise from beginning to end, your Majesty," I answered.

"Good," he said, and then, as my Military Cross was handed him, he affixed it to my tunic and said :

"Lieutenant Fallon, we deeply thank you for your services and I hope you live many years to wear the decoration I have placed upon you."

With that I stepped back the directed two paces, bowed and left by the right door, returned to the salon, received my cap and